CHRISTIAN HEROES: THEN & NOW

IDA SCUDDER

Healing Bodies, Touching Hearts

JANET & GEOFF BENGE

YWAM PUBLISHING

P.O. BOX 55787   SEATTLE,

T0019913

YWAM Publishing is the publishing ministry of Youth With A Mission (YWAM), an international missionary organization of Christians from many denominations dedicated to presenting Jesus Christ to this generation. To this end, YWAM has focused its efforts in three main areas: (1) training and equipping believers for their part in fulfilling the Great Commission (Matthew 28:19), (2) personal evangelism, and (3) mercy ministry (medical and relief work).

For a free catalog of books and materials, call (425) 771-1153 or (800) 922-2143. Visit us online at www.ywampublishing.com.

Ida Scudder: Healing Bodies, Touching Hearts
Copyright © 2003 by YWAM Publishing

Published by YWAM Publishing
a ministry of Youth With A Mission
P.O. Box 55787, Seattle, WA 98155-0787

All rights reserved. No part of this book may be reproduced in any form without permission in writing from the publisher, except in the case of brief quotations in critical articles or reviews.

Library of Congress Cataloging-in-Publication Data
Benge, Janet, 1958–
Ida Scudder, healing bodies, touching hearts / by Janet and Geoff Benge.
p. cm.—(Christian heroes, then & now)
     Includes bibliographical references.
     ISBN 1-57658-285-X
     1. Scudder, Ida Sophia, 1870-1960—Juvenile literature. 2. Missionaries, Medical—India—Juvenile literature. [1. Scudder, Ida Sophia, 1870–1960. 2. Missionaries. 3. Physicians. 4. Women—Biography.] I. Benge, Geoff, 1954- II. Title. III. Series.
     R722.32.S37B46 2003
     610'.92—dc21   2003008859

ISBN 978-1-57658-285-5 (paperback)
ISBN 978-1-57658-601-3 (ebook)

Sixth printing 2021

Printed in the United States of America

CHRISTIAN HEROES: THEN & NOW

IDA SCUDDER

Healing Bodies, Touching Hearts

CHRISTIAN HEROES: THEN & NOW

Adoniram Judson	Isobel Kuhn
Albert Schweitzer	Jacob DeShazer
Amy Carmichael	Jim Elliot
Betty Greene	John Flynn
Brother Andrew	John Newton
Cameron Townsend	John Wesley
Charles Mulli	John Williams
Clarence Jones	Jonathan Goforth
Corrie ten Boom	Klaus-Dieter John
Count Zinzendorf	Lillian Trasher
C. S. Lewis	Loren Cunningham
C. T. Studd	Lottie Moon
David Bussau	Mary Slessor
David Livingstone	Mildred Cable
Dietrich Bonhoeffer	Nate Saint
D. L. Moody	Norman Grubb
Elisabeth Elliot	Paul Brand
Eric Liddell	Rachel Saint
Florence Young	Richard Wurmbrand
Francis Asbury	Rowland Bingham
George Müller	Samuel Zwemer
Gladys Aylward	Sundar Singh
Helen Roseveare	Wilfred Grenfell
Hudson Taylor	William Booth
Ida Scudder	William Carey

Available in paperback, e-book, and audiobook formats. Unit study curriculum guides are available for select biographies.

www.YWAMpublishing.com

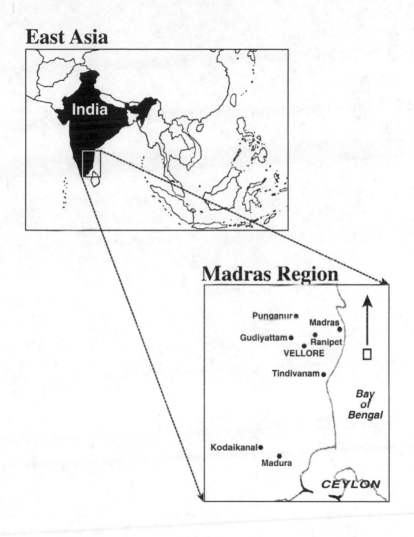

Contents

Chapter 1

"The Devil Is Coming!"

Ida Scudder buttoned a long coat over her white doctor uniform. She then secured a veil over her hat to keep out the dust and headed outside. In front of the small hospital that she oversaw sat the brand-new 1909 Peugeot motorcar. Salomi, her assistant, and a female Bible teacher were already seated in the back seat of the vehicle. Around them was packed all the medical equipment they needed to run the Roadsides, the outpatient clinics they held in the villages that surrounded Vellore in southern India. Since no space was left inside the car, canvas bags packed with drugs and bandages dangled from either side of the windshield.

Ida had to admit that it looked quite a sight as she stepped onto the running board and into the front seat. Hussain, the driver, waved enthusiastically from in front of the car. He bent down and turned the crank. A cloud of oily gray smoke belched from the exhaust pipe as the single-cylinder engine burst to life and the car vibrated violently. Hussain climbed in behind the wheel, adjusted his goggles, and released the brake, and they were off.

Ida said a quick prayer for their safety. She felt she needed to because until a few days ago Hussain had never even seen a motorcar, let alone driven one. He had made a few practice runs around the hospital perimeter and declared himself ready to take Ida to her weekly mobile clinics.

"Look out!" Ida yelled as an oxcart stacked high with bags of rice loomed in front of them.

Hussain grinned and pulled on the steering wheel, sending the car careening toward a ditch. The bags of bandages bounced against the windshield, and Salomi screamed from the backseat. Schoolchildren ran for cover.

Hussain let out a whoop and tugged the steering wheel in the other direction. The car swung back the other way, narrowly missing the cart as they passed it. The startled driver pulled his oxen to a halt. Hussain waved cheerfully and put his foot on the accelerator.

"Slow down!" Ida demanded.

Crestfallen, Hussain eased his foot off the gas pedal. Eventually he managed to negotiate his way through the streets and out into the country toward the first Roadside.

The car had just rounded a corner when a group of field workers walking along the road turned and saw it. Ida watched as the men dropped their scythes and ran off into the fields. "The devil is coming! The devil is coming!" the men screamed.

Ida ordered Hussain to stop the car, and she ran into the field after the workers.

"We will not harm you!" she yelled. "It is us, the same people who come to help you every week."

"It's a devil. Look how it breathes smoke. An animal-less cart is bad magic!" one man yelled over his shoulder as he kept running.

Ida gave up the chase. Who could blame the men? This was the first motorcar they had ever seen, and Ida supposed it was shocking to them. She hoped in time to prove that the car was no devil. Rather, it would enable her to bring life-changing medical help to many more Indian people. Before the arrival of the car, it had taken her three times as long to get out into the country, and the bumpy rides on the lumbering, springless oxcarts had left Ida bruised and sore. She wished her father were sitting in the car beside her; he would have loved it. He had always looked for better and more efficient ways to serve the Indian people.

Ida smiled and shook her head in astonishment as her thoughts drifted back to her parents and her childhood. She could hardly believe that these medical trips into the Indian countryside were now part of her life. Ida had been born in India, where her father, and his father before him, had served as a medical missionary. Growing up, Ida had been sure of one thing: she would never follow in her father's footsteps. In fact she was angry whenever anyone suggested it. Instead she had wanted to spend the rest of her life in the United States, keeping the horrible images of dying Indians and starving children as far away as possible.

But now here she was, living and working in India as a missionary doctor. As the car bumped along the curvy dirt road, Ida smiled again in amazement. She never could have foreseen the strange set of circumstances God would use to lead her back to India, or the unexpected twists and turns along the way.

Chapter 2

A Better Place to Live

"Ida, come here. Mama needs you." Ida heard the call from her hiding place behind the big water jar in the kitchen. She peeked out and saw her mother walking toward the door. Something about the way her mother walked made Ida pay attention instead of turning the search for her into a game. Ida slipped out from behind the jar and followed her mother.

As she stepped out the door, Ida was shocked to see hundreds of small children being marched into the backyard. As the children entered the yard, Ida's two older brothers organized them to sit in rows.

"There you are," Sophia Scudder, Ida's mother, exclaimed, putting her hand on her daughter's shoulder. "Come with me. You can be in charge of feeding the children. Give them one chunk of bread each. That's all they can have. Can you do that?"

Six-year-old Ida nodded, though in truth she was very confused. Her mother had never before put her in charge of anything, much less feeding hundreds of children younger than she was.

With a brisk efficiency that served her well as a busy doctor's wife, Mrs. Scudder showed Ida the basket filled with broken chunks of bread.

"Start at the front," she said, "and when you have fed a whole row, wave to Walter or Henry, and they will escort the children out the gate. Charlie will stand guard to make sure they don't come in again. There is only enough food for one piece each. There are government guards outside to make sure no adults get in, as we have only enough to feed the children. Do you understand?" She knelt down beside her daughter, and Ida could see the tears in her mother's eyes. "Just one piece each because otherwise there won't be enough to go around."

Sophia Scudder carried the huge wicker basket outside, where Ida began dipping into it and handing out the bread. Ida could barely look at the children she was feeding. They had the same deep brown eyes and flashing white teeth as the other Indian children she played with here in the village of Vellore, where her father was a doctor and a pastor. But unlike her playmates, the children in front of her had protruding stomachs and stick-thin arms and legs. As Ida moved down the rows, the children eagerly grabbed for the food.

Ida recalled how Walter had complained about there being no rice for dinner one night the week before. Her father had explained that there was a famine in India and many children did not have enough food to eat. Now, crowded into the backyard of the Scudder clinic were some of those starving children.

Ida would rather have been doing just about anything other than handing out the bread, not because she did not care that a famine was killing people but because she cared too much. She imagined herself in the place of the children, begging for tiny pieces of food that would not satisfy her.

Finally the breadbasket was empty, and the remaining children drifted out the gate.

"Come back tomorrow," Ida's brother Henry told them. "We will have more food then."

That night at the dinner table, Ida felt guilty eating her rice and vegetable curry.

"Thank you for your help today, children," Dr. Scudder said, looking around the table at his sons, John, Lewis, Henry, Charlie, and Walter, and his daughter, Ida. "We are going to need you again tomorrow. I have decided to set up a relief camp here at Vellore. We've sent for cartloads of rice and clothing from Madras, but that's a hundred miles away and will take days to get here. Until then we are going to have to do the best we can. Your mother is going to be in charge of feeding and clothing the refugees while I tend to their medical needs. School will be suspended until the famine is over; there is just too much to do."

Ida and Walter exchanged glances. Nothing had ever been serious enough in the past to interfere with the daily lessons their mother prepared for them.

As Ida lay in bed later that night, she could hear workers lashing bamboo together to make shelters for the hundreds of people already pouring into the relief center. She wondered how long the famine, and the lack of rain during the monsoon season that had caused it, would last.

The next Sunday Ida went to church with her family. Her father preached the sermon as usual, and her mother stayed afterward to talk with the young mothers in the congregation. Ida and her nanny, Mary Ayah, also stayed behind, and when Ida's mother was finished, the three of them made the short trip back to the house in a bullock-drawn cart called a *bandy*. It was a very hot day, and the collar of Ida's starched white dress dug into her neck. While Ida was trying to loosen the collar without her mother's noticing, Mary suddenly exclaimed, "Ayoh! Look at those children!"

Ida turned her head in the direction Mary was pointing. Two children, about six years old, were lying at the side of the road. They had their arms around each other.

"Why aren't they moving?" Ida asked.

"They're not moving because they're dead," Ida's nanny replied matter-of-factly.

"Mary Ayah!" Mrs. Scudder scolded. "That was not necessary."

Ida looked away from the scene, but it was too late. The image of the two dead children was seared in her mind. She no longer looked forward to the dinner the cook was preparing for the family. All around her were starving people, and even the coconut and mango trees were beginning to die from lack of water.

Often, when Dr. Scudder returned from the hundred or so villages under his care, Ida would hear him and her mother in whispered conversation. Ida knew they were trying to keep the worst of the famine from her, but the stories she overheard terrified her. One time, when her father was taking two thousand rupees in silver coins to town to buy relief supplies, bandits attacked him. He did not carry a gun, but he pulled a long, black cigar out of his pocket and aimed it at the bandits. In the twilight they mistook the cigar for a firearm and fled without the silver. Another time, her father visited a village and found that the entire population had died, some of starvation and others from the dreaded disease cholera that was sweeping through the nation. Her father said that even the village cattle and dogs lay still on the ground.

Ida continued to help out as best she could, but she couldn't relieve the strain her parents were under. Finally, in October 1877, the rains began to fall, and her father predicted that the first rice crops would be harvested by Christmas.

When the death toll from the famine and the cholera epidemic was finally tallied, more than three million people had died. Ida knew that her whole family had done all they could to help, but she was deeply affected to discover how many helpless people had died.

By the following April, Dr. Scudder's health was in perilous condition. Various tropical diseases had so weakened his body over the sixteen years he had served in India that he now needed to return to the United States to recover.

The thought of going "home" to America was very strange to Ida, who was nearly seven and a half years old by now. Her two oldest brothers, John and Lewis, were eager to attend a proper school there, but Ida was not so sure. She wondered what America was really like. She knew she had lots of relatives in the United States and that her mother's parents lived there. But as much as her family was rooted in the United States, the family tree also twined around southern India.

Ida had heard the story often enough—it was practically a legend. Her father's father, Dr. John Scudder I, was a successful young doctor in New York City when in 1819 a patient gave him a pamphlet titled *The Claims of Six Hundred Millions*. The pamphlet was about the people of Asia and how most of them had never heard the gospel. As John Scudder read the pamphlet, he became convinced that he should go to Ceylon as a medical missionary. His wife, Harriet, Ida's grandmother, agreed to go with him, and so he applied to be the first medical missionary ever to go out from the United States to a foreign land. He was accepted to go but at great personal cost. His own father disagreed so violently with his decision to be a missionary that he cut John out of his will and announced he never wanted to see his son again.

John and Harriet Scudder went to Ceylon and then on to India. Their first three children died from heat-related illnesses, but the Scudders went on to raise ten more children, eight sons and two daughters. Ida's father, John Scudder II, was their second youngest child.

Seven of the sons, Henry, William, Joseph, Ezekiel, Jared, Silas, and John, returned to the United States for their education and then returned "home" to India. All of them were qualified doctors of medicine as well as pastors, and two of them earned doctorates of divinity. The eighth son, Samuel, would have joined them, but he drowned while he was a student in theological college. The two daughters, Harriet and Louisa, both married Englishmen who also served in India. Now various cousins of Ida's were beginning to trickle back from college in America to take their place in the ranks of Scudder missionaries in India. Among them were Dr. Harry and Bessie Scudder, cousins who had married each other and had come to Vellore to take Ida's father's place at the medical clinic.

The trip to the United States was the first sea voyage Ida had ever undertaken. She had been born at the mission hospital in Ranipet, India, on December 9, 1870, and had spent her entire life in southern India.

On the voyage to America, Ida's mother taught her to knit and told her stories. Ida loved to hear about her parents' voyage to India seventeen years before. James Buchanan had been president when they left. The first news they heard from home when they landed in Madras was that Abraham Lincoln had been elected president, Fort Sumter in South Carolina had been bombarded by Confederate troops, and the Civil War had begun.

The ocean voyage itself had lasted four long months, since they had sailed around the Cape of Good Hope at the southern tip of Africa and then across the Indian ocean to India. They had been out of sight of land nearly all of the way. Ida's mother, who had been born and raised in Ohio, had found the seascape unsettling and depressing. To make matters worse, the ship had been delayed for two weeks by lack of wind. Ida's first voyage to the United States, however, was not nearly as long as her parents' voyage to India had been. Two months after setting out, the ship arrived in New York harbor, and Ida soon set her feet on American soil.

The first thing Ida noticed about the United States was how well fed everyone looked, and the second was how many other people had blue eyes and pale blond hair like hers. She could walk all the way down the street from the boarding house to the church without one person reaching out to pull her hair to see whether it was real.

John Scudder decided he needed country air to recover fully. Much to Ida's amazement, the family moved to a farm in Nebraska, where her father took up practice as a country doctor.

Once she adjusted to the changed scenery, Ida was happy in Nebraska. She loved the family's horse, the wide-open fields, and the flat landscape.

And as the days rolled by, she came to the conclusion that America was a lot better place to live than India. No one was starving or wore rags, neighbors helped each other, and the countryside smelled sweet compared with the stench of the market in Vellore on a hot afternoon. By the time she had been in the United States for three years, Ida had made herself a promise: no matter what, she would never live in India again.

Chapter 3

"I Will Make My Own Way in the World"

In 1883 twelve-year-old Ida Scudder learned that her father was returning to missionary work in India. John Scudder told Ida that initially he would go alone to see whether he was strong enough to survive the hot climate. Then, if all went well, Ida's mother would join him in a year or so. In the meantime Ida's brother Lewis would take over running the farm in Nebraska so that Mrs. Scudder and the three youngest children could continue to live there.

Life was just not the same for Ida without her father around. She found herself becoming increasingly resentful of the fact that so many members of her family were missionaries. She became even more upset two years later when she learned that her mother was going to be joining her father in India

25

and Ida was to be sent to live with her Uncle Henry and Aunt Fanny in Chicago. Uncle Henry was her father's oldest brother, and he had retired from missionary life in India twenty years before because of ill health.

Up until this time Ida had never been separated from her mother, not even for so much as a night. The thought of being on different continents from her parents filled her with dread. To make matters worse, when the day arrived for her mother to leave, it was raining heavily and the adults decided that it would be unwise for Ida to accompany her mother to the train station. Instead Ida was left to watch through the upstairs window as her mother disappeared from view in a carriage. When the carriage was out of sight, Ida flung herself down onto the bed and wept into her mother's pillow. The smell of her mother's perfume on it only increased her sadness.

Slowly Ida adjusted to the idea of being alone in the United States. Her uncle and aunt were kind to her, although they were much sterner than her parents. However, the return of Ida's mother to India stirred up long-buried dreams in Uncle Henry, who eventually announced that he, too, was going to look for a way to resume missionary work. As a concession to his poor health, he set his sights on Japan rather than India.

By 1886 Dr. Henry Scudder had made all of the arrangements for his new work in Japan except for one thing—what to do with his niece. Ida, for her part, did not have the slightest idea what should happen to her next. She was torn between wanting to be with her parents and the dread of setting foot in India.

The problem was finally solved when a well-known preacher named Dwight L. Moody came to dinner. Mr. Moody described a seminary for girls that he had founded in his birthplace of Northfield, Massachusetts. By the time the meal was over, it was settled. Ida would go to Northfield and attend the seminary. Ida loved Northfield from the start. The Connecticut River ran through the small town, and when Ida arrived in the fall of 1886, the trees were a blaze of autumn colors.

For the first time in her life, Ida was surrounded by girls her own age, and she made up her mind to enjoy every minute of her time at the school. She found schoolwork easy, which gave her plenty of time to spend playing silly tricks on her classmates and teachers. She soon paired up with another high-spirited girl, named Florence Updyke. If anything went wrong in the East Hall of the seminary, it could inevitably be traced back to the two of them. On one occasion, when homework was particularly boring, Ida spied the horse and carriage of a visiting German teacher tied up in front of the school. She convinced Florence to join her, and the two girls crept up to the horse and carriage, unhitched them, and led them away. Once they were out of sight of the seminary, the girls climbed onto the carriage and went for a joyride. When they finally tired of joyriding, they tied the horse and carriage to a tree about two miles from school and hiked back in time for dinner.

When the two girls were summoned to the headmistress's office after dinner, neither of them could keep a straight face. As a result of their actions, they were assigned to kitchen duty for weeks afterward. Still, whenever they saw each other clad in their aprons in the kitchen, they burst into giggles.

Later on, a larger group of the girls, the "bunch" as they were called, devised a game whereby everyone had to collect some item from somewhere in the school and meet in the furnace room to explain the daring way she had come by her object. The girls took turns gleefully recounting how they had "borrowed" a pot from under the cook's nose, a pen from the headmistress's private desk, and even the screws from the hinge in the seminary's front gate! Of course, the greater challenge became putting the items back undetected.

On Thanksgiving Day during her second year at the school, Ida and some of her friends decided to go into the nearby town of Brattleboro for dinner. On the way they met up with some boys from Mount Hermon School. Although the girls of Northfield were forbidden to mix with the boys of Mount Hermon, except at specially chaperoned school events, the group decided to have dinner together. They were halfway through their turkey dinner when the English teacher at Northfield

Seminary walked into the dining room. The girls, their faces white with fear, turned to Ida.

"Don't worry," Ida whispered. "Let's enjoy the meal, and I'll think of some way out of it."

The meal went on, and by the time it was over, Ida had a plan. She stopped at a florist on the way back to school and bought the biggest bunch of flowers that were for sale. She wrote a note to the English teacher, thanking her for allowing them to have such a nice Thanksgiving dinner with those well-mannered young men who insisted they join them at the dinner table, and she left the note and flowers in the teacher's office.

Ida was soon summoned to the English teacher's office, but her plan worked, and she got away with just a warning not to mix with the boys again. As Ida left the room, she was sure she saw a slight smile on the teacher's face.

For Ida's fourth Christmas at Northfield Seminary, one of Ida's aunts sent her a diary as a gift. Ida was soon filling its pages with accounts of her adventures and run-ins with authorities. On January 11, 1890, she wrote:

> This evening Spook [Florence], Annie, Bessie, Mittle and I were going to have a big time having cream, coffee and lobster but as we had prayer meeting in chapel ending the week of prayer, we only had fifteen minutes and so couldn't have our fun. Spook and I

went into the attic and smoked cubebs [cigars] and had a great time over them.

Two days later Ida was complaining in her diary:

Miss Ford went for me for whistling again. She called me into the office and talked to me about having coffee and cocoa and said that I had done wrong to take that oil stove [another prank].

Ida was well behaved for a while, but on March 3 her entry read:

Over a month since I last took my pen to write, and much has happened. One day about the 20th of Feb. Edna Skinner and I got to laughing in chapel and oh how I was squelched by Miss Hall. She very kindly told me I had been a stumbling block to some and would still be if I did not do things differently.

Still, Ida found it impossible not to get into mischief of one sort or another. As her four years at seminary slipped by, Ida wondered what she would do next. It was not a question many of her friends had to ask. Most of them were from wealthy families and had come to Northfield to round out their education before a "stepping-out" party and the proposal of marriage that normally followed. But Ida had no parents in America and no one who was interested in sponsoring her stepping-out party. Somehow, though, she would work it out so that she could step out and catch the eye of some very rich and handsome young bachelor.

Much to Ida's dismay, her parents assumed that she would return to India to become a missionary. Ida had not yet found the right words to tell them she had no intention of doing any such thing, especially after the grim letters she had received from them.

One of the letters Ida received from her father at the end of 1889 started,

> We are in the midst of our hot weather and it is fearful, I don't think I have ever fretted more over it. If it is dry I do not mind so much, but in this place which is not very far from the sea, the air is full of moisture and consequently the evaporation is less, so that we are in a reeking sweat most of the time.

Her father went on to explain that the thermometer read 102 degrees Fahrenheit in the shade and did not fall below 86 degrees at night. Ida recoiled when she read such descriptions. Just how was a lady supposed to keep her hair perfectly curled and her dress immaculate in such conditions?

In 1890 Ida received another message from her father, though this time it was not a letter but a telegram. One Saturday afternoon Ida was called from her room to receive the telegram. It was the first telegram she had ever received, and her hands shook as she split open the envelope and took out the telegram, which read, "COME IMMEDIATELY. YOUR MOTHER ILL AND NEEDS YOU."

Ida stared at the message. Her mother was ill? How ill? Would she ever see her again? Suddenly all of Ida's resolve never to set foot in India again melted away, and she calculated how long it would take to make the voyage to Madras. She knew that her brother Henry was due to set sail for India, where he was going to take over the boys' school their father had founded. Ida decided the two of them could travel together.

When Ida told her friends about her plan to go to India, Florence teased her mercilessly. "You will go to India and end up as a missionary just like all the other Scudders, and we will never see you again."

Ida felt the anger rising in her. She stamped her foot. "I will not!" she retorted. "I am going to spend one year in India, just one year. Then I am going to come back to America and live. So don't any of you say I will be a missionary, because I won't—never, ever, ever."

On July 30, 1890, Ida stood beside Henry on the deck of the *City of Berlin*. She held a bouquet of roses that her classmates from Northfield had sent as a farewell gift to the New York pier the ship departed from. As she smelled the roses, Ida tried not to think of the dirt and awful smells she recalled from her childhood in India. Could it really be over twelve years since she had left there? It felt so strange to be going back with her brother at her side.

The voyage was fast and uneventful, and on September 20 the *City of Berlin* docked in Madras. Ida knew her father would be waiting for them at the foot of the gangplank, but when she got off the ship, she walked right past him! In the eight years since she had seen him, he had grown into an old man, and she did not recognize him. It was only when Henry yelled out, "Father," that Ida turned to see Dr. Scudder beaming with joy.

Soon their luggage was assembled, and Ida watched as it was loaded onto the train bound for Tindivanam. It felt strange to be back in India. Once again Ida saw turbaned men and sari-clad women in the streets. Pungent odors filled the air. And there was the heat. After four years in Massachusetts, Ida felt like she was suffocating. She dabbed perspiration from her forehead with a handkerchief that was soon saturated. And then there was the crowd. People teemed around them as they made their way onto the train.

Once the Scudders were seated on the train, Ida had the opportunity to study her father closely. His beard had turned from black to white, and he was thinner than she remembered him. Still, as she looked into his dark brown eyes, she could see the father she had known.

He must have guessed what Ida was thinking, because he wistfully said, "It's been a long time, hasn't it, Ida? Your mother and I have missed so much of your growing-up years. Just imagine, you will be twenty in two months."

Ida felt herself turning red with anger. She wanted to blurt out, *Whose fault was it that you missed so much of my growing-up years?* After all, it was her father who had chosen mission work over keeping the family together, and as far as Ida was concerned, she had paid the greatest price for that decision.

Green rice fields flashed by as Ida stared out the train window. She could see huge rock formations rising from the otherwise flat countryside. She counted the oxen she saw—…five…six…seven. She did whatever it took to keep her mind off the loneliness she had felt away from her parents over the years. *Somehow,* she vowed, *I will get through this year, and then I will make my own way in the world.*

Chapter 4

Together Again

The train pulled into the station at Tindivanam. Ida looked down with dismay at her blue muslin dress. It had been the latest fashion when she bought it in New York, but now it looked like something fished out of a ragbag. It was dusty and soaked with perspiration; even the muttonchop sleeves looked like deflated balloons. Ida hated the thought of meeting her mother looking like this, but as it turned out, her mother was not at the station to meet them.

After they had clambered off the train, Dr. Scudder hired a bandy, the familiar oxcart, to take them to the mission hospital where her parents now lived.

Ida's heart beat fast as she wondered how her mother would look. Would she be strong enough to

35

come out and greet them or be languishing in bed? Since Ida was too afraid to ask her father, she had to wait and see for herself.

The bandy ride seemed to last forever as the cart lumbered through the dusty countryside. All around them Indian people stopped to stare at the white doctor with his two grown children.

"We're nearly home!" Dr. Scudder finally announced. "See that tamarind tree? It's just in front of the house."

Ida peered down the street at the huge tree. In one unladylike movement, she jumped from the slow-moving bandy. As she raced down the road, a whitewashed building with a thatched roof and long veranda came into view. Standing on the veranda was a white woman.

Ida yelled, "Marmee! Marmee!" and held out her arms as she ran. Then, all of a sudden, she felt strangely self-conscious. She stopped running and swept her hands through her hair. This time it was her mother who rushed forward, and soon the two were embracing—mother and daughter together again after five long years.

Soon Ida and Henry and their parents were all sitting on the veranda drinking tea and eating the vaguely familiar sweet cakes that Mrs. Scudder reminded Ida had been her favorite food as a little girl. When afternoon tea was over, Ida's mother had to return to bed. She had used up all of her strength welcoming her children.

The following evening, after Ida had unpacked everything and settled into her room, she flopped down on the bed and opened her diary. The entries she had made at Northfield felt a million miles away now. She picked up her pencil and wrote, "I have been in India for two whole days. Our house—" she looked at the word *our* and then crossed it out; there was no point in getting used to it. She wrote on, "My parents' house is on a big mission compound near a school. It is made of sun-baked bricks plastered with mud, then whitewashed. It has three rooms in a row."

Ida paused for a moment and went on, determined to describe the place so that she could picture it when she returned to America. "The thatched roof is full of white ants, and every now and then drops down dust on your head. But we—" she stopped and drew a determined black line through the word *we*. "My parents are going to move into a new bungalow."

For Ida life soon fell into a routine, and she found she enjoyed the daily challenges it presented. Besides being the only doctor in the area, her father was the principal of a boarding school for nearly one hundred boys, which her brother Henry had come to take over. Half of the boys in the school were the sons of Christian converts from the neighboring villages, and the other half were Hindus whose parents were eager for them to have the best education possible. Ida's mother had overseen the daily running of the school, buying the food, setting the menu, seeing that the laundry was done properly, and ordering clothes and supplies for the boys. But now that she was sick, this responsibility had fallen to Ida. It took her several weeks to recall enough Tamil to communicate effectively with the cook and the maids, but she found a lot could be achieved with hand signals. Sometimes she brought the cook into her mother's room, where the three of them would work out the menu and the supplies that would be needed.

Sometimes when Ida was alone with her mother, Sophia Scudder would pat her daughter's hand and say, "It is so good to have you here, dear. You cannot imagine what it is like to have no one to speak English with from one month to the next. Your father is here, of course, but he is gone for two or three weeks at a time on the circuit touring Christian churches. How wonderful it is to have my daughter back to stay. I am getting quite used to it."

Ida hated to hear those words. It made her dread the day when she would have to tell her parents that she did not intend to stay in India and that as soon as her mother was stronger, she would be heading back to the United States to make a life for herself. She waited for just the right time to say this, but it never seemed to come.

Thankfully, Mrs. Scudder began to recover from her illness, and four months after Ida's arrival, she was well enough to resume many of her former responsibilities, leaving Ida free to accompany her father on a special evangelistic mission. Ida's Uncle Jared and his daughter Dixie were also going along.

Ida was glad to accompany her father. Dixie, who was six years older, was one of Ida's favorite cousins.

Since Uncle Jared and his family lived at Vellore, fifty miles north of Tindivanam, they all agreed to meet each other for the mission halfway between the two towns. Once they met up, they began to hold a series of open-air meetings in a number of villages.

There was plenty to be done, and Ida and Dixie soon teamed up. Together they went to visit the local women. As in most areas around Vellore, about 10 percent of the families were Muslim and 90 percent were Hindu. Ida and Dixie set off first to visit the Muslim women. Both the Muslim women and the Hindu women rarely left the courtyards of their homes. In fact, some had not even seen the street outside their homes for many years. Instead they stayed indoors cooking and tending to the needs of their families. This meant that many of the women were eager to have visitors, especially foreign visitors like Ida and Dixie, who could tell them stories about what was going on in the world far beyond the courtyards of their homes.

During these visits Dixie did most of the talking, telling the women Bible stories and urging them to consider sending their children to the Christian schools in the area.

Sometimes the two cousins also spent time in small village churches preparing children to be baptized, assisting Ida's father as he examined patients, and teaching the catechism to others.

One thing seemed to flow into the next. After an open-air meeting, where Ida's father and uncle would take turns preaching from the back of a bandy, Dr.

Scudder would lay a white sheet on the ground and proceed with minor operations, assisted by Uncle Jared. Broken arms and legs were set, growths removed, abscesses lanced, and teeth pulled. Ida was always fascinated as her father and uncle tied up their beards and invited the patients to lie down on the sheet. Invariably a crowd would gather around, making comments on every procedure. Of course, only men could be operated on in this way, because Hindu husbands would not allow another man, not even a doctor, to see their wives without their clothes on, including their veils. The whole idea seemed ludicrous to Ida as she watched her father try to diagnose a woman's problem by feeling the pulse at her wrist through a nearly closed door.

After watching Dixie for several days, Ida marveled at how she kept working so cheerfully, even for Uncle Jared, who barked out orders and never smiled. Dixie was a very beautiful woman. She was rumored to have had more marriage proposals than any other white woman in India. Ida wondered why she had not accepted one of these proposals and gotten out from under her father's incessant commands.

One day, when they had some spare time, Ida and Dixie managed to slip out of the camp and go for a walk alongside a stream, where they found a huge oleander bush in full bloom. Delighted by the sight of the oleander, Dixie and Ida picked the blossoms and festooned their hats with them. They then gathered branches from the bush and headed back to camp laughing and giggling at the sight of each other's hat.

Back at camp Dixie led the way into the tent, with Ida right behind. Just as Ida stepped inside, she caught a glimpse of her Uncle Jared. His face was as stormy as thunder clouds. "Take those flowers off! Both of you!" he boomed. "What do you think you are doing? We are here to inspire holiness in Christians, not this—this frivolity."

Much to Ida's dismay, Dixie replied meekly, "Yes, Father," as she unwound the rose-colored blossoms from her hat. Ida waited for her father to say something, but he continued working quietly in the corner.

Finally Ida stepped outside the tent, indignation rising within her. *How dare Uncle Jared speak to us like that? What kind of Christianity is it that does not allow a girl to put a flower in her hat?* she fumed as she pulled more blooms from the oleander branches they had picked and stuck them deliberately into her hat. She did not stop until the entire brim and bowl of the hat were completely covered. *That will teach the old grouch,* she told herself, pulling her hat on again and walking back into the tent, her chin held high.

Both men looked up in silence as she entered, and Ida thought she saw the beginnings of a smile on her father's face. But Uncle Jared's eyes looked like they would pop with anger. He opened his mouth to say something and then suddenly burst into a fit of laughter. He did not stop until tears were rolling down his cheeks. He turned to Ida's father, who was also laughing, and said, "Well, brother, that's what comes from having five sons and only one daughter. She's much too independent minded. I don't envy you one bit."

Ida did not know what to say. She wished Dixie would seize the opportunity and jam some flowers into her hat once again, but she did not.

That night, when the two cousins were lying on their cots, Ida wondered what Dixie really thought about having to do everything her father said. Didn't she ever feel like telling him to mind his own business? Her heart beat fast as she worked up the courage to ask Dixie.

"Do you really like doing what your father says all the time?" she finally asked. "Don't you have your own dreams—things you want to do without anyone else bossing you around?"

"Oh, yes!" Dixie replied.

Ida was startled by the passion in her cousin's voice. Perhaps Dixie did have some spunk after all. Perhaps she also longed to escape India. Perhaps the two of them could return to America together and make something of their lives.

"Tell me what your dream is," Ida urged. "What is it you want to do more than anything?"

Dixie rolled over, and Ida could see her eyes sparkling in the candlelight. "If I could do anything I liked…" Dixie said in a dreamy voice. "Well…I don't know if you would understand."

"I certainly would," Ida whispered back. "I've lived other places besides here, you know."

"Yes, I know," Dixie replied. "It's just that…well …if I could do anything I liked, I would find the smallest, dirtiest village in the whole province, and I would live there in a tent or a simple hut. I would work with the women of the village to teach them hygiene and how to look after their babies so they don't get sick. And I'd start a Sunday school for the children. More than anything else, that's what I want to do."

Ida lay still in bed. She dared not open her mouth for fear she would laugh out loud. What kind of crazy dream was that? And from one of the prettiest girls in all of India! Dixie certainly needed a trip back to the United States before it was too late and she decided to spend the rest of her life in this dirty, smelly country.

During the rest of the evangelistic campaign, Ida took great pains to avoid having any more serious conversations with Dixie. It was far too disturbing to listen to someone she admired describe how she wanted to throw her life away.

When Ida got back to Tindivanam, a letter was waiting for her from Annie Hancock, one of her friends from school in Northfield. Ida ripped open the letter, eager to read some of the gossip that seemed a million miles away from her now.

As usual, though, Annie couldn't help making the letter religious. She asked Ida if she had preached to the women and children yet, or if she was able to read the Bible in Tamil. She gushed about how blessed Ida was to be able to bring "light and truth to places of darkness and ignorance." Ida shook her head as she read. Did her friend really think that coming to India would have changed her that much? She shook her head again and promised herself she would write back to Annie that night. Someone needed to tell Annie that being a missionary was not the wonderful career she imagined it to be, and it was certainly not one that Ida intended to pursue.

It was not the letter that Ida wrote back to Annie that night that would forever change her world. Rather, it was the strange events that occurred while she wrote it.

Chapter 5

"There Is Something I Can Do about It"

Before she went to bed, Ida sat down to write a letter to her friend Annie. She settled herself at her desk and began writing.

> Dear Annie, I am sitting in my room with your letter in front of me. It is late at night, and the compound is so quiet I can almost hear a *palli* (that's a lizard) darting up the wall to catch a bug. My father is working in his bedroom-study next door, and my mother, I hope, is asleep.

Ida paused for a moment and dipped her pen in the inkwell. That was enough chitchat. It was time to tell Annie how she felt about missionary work. She continued:

> You say you wish you could be a mission-
> ary like me. *Don't say that!* I'm not a mission-
> ary and never will be. But you're not like me.
> You always were more—more spiritual, Annie
> darling. You might really like it here. I can see
> you going into the *zenanas* (women's quarters
> in Indian homes) and visiting the little wives
> and mothers. Some of them have to live all
> their lives within four walls, and they're so
> young, Annie, not near as old as you and I…

A faint cough interrupted Ida's flow of words. Someone was outside her door. This did not alarm Ida; people came at all hours of the day and night to get her father. She put down her pen, picked up the desk lamp, and walked to the door and opened it.

Sure enough, a young Indian man stood on the far side of the veranda. Ida recognized him immediately as one of Tindivanam's most respected Brahmans, a member of the highest caste among India's Hindus. The man bowed his head slightly, and his white turban bobbed up and down.

"What do you need?" Ida asked.

The man stepped forward, and Ida could see he was shaking.

"Are you sick?" she asked.

"No, not me," he said. "It is my wife. You must come to her. She is only fourteen, and this is her first baby. It will not come out, and the barber woman says that she is going to die. But..." his voice trembled with emotion, "she must not die, *Ammal* [honored friend]! She is a beautiful girl. They told me that you are from America and that you can help her."

"No, no," Ida said soothingly as she gathered the hem of her dress. "But come with me. I will take you to my father. He is the doctor, and I am sure he will know what to do." Ida turned to lead the way to her father's study. But the Brahman man did not follow, and Ida looked to see what was keeping him. Much to her surprise he stood still, his face in his hands.

"All is lost," he said. "I cannot take a man into my house to care for my wife. No man other than those of her own family has so much as seen her face. You don't know what you are saying."

"But my father can help," Ida exclaimed. "You said that without help she will die. Don't you understand? Come, let's go and talk to my father."

"*I* don't understand!" yelled the man. "It is *you* who do not understand. My wife cannot be defiled. If you cannot help me, I will go."

"No, wait one minute," Ida said, hurrying off to get her father. Surely he would know how to talk some sense into this Brahman. She burst into her father's office and quickly told him what had happened. The two of them went out to talk to their visitor. Dr. Scudder tried to convince the man that a doctor seeing a patient is a different matter from a man looking at a woman.

"If what you tell me is true, it sounds like your wife will die without my help," Ida's father concluded.

The man nodded. "If that is what must be, then it must be. But it is such a shame, Ammal," he said. Once again looking at Ida he added, "Are you sure you will not come?"

Ida shook her head. "It would be of no use. I have no skills in delivering babies. I would be no better than the barber's wife."

"Then so be it. I apologize for disturbing your evening."

With that the man turned and stepped off the veranda. Ida could hear the crunch of his footsteps on the stone sidewalk. Anger seethed within her. She looked at her father in the lamplight.

"Why? How could he be so selfish?" she demanded.

Dr. Scudder sighed. "You know as well as I do, Ida, it is the way in India. A Brahman does not let any man see his wife's face, much less attend her as she gives birth to a child."

"I know that," Ida spat back, "but this is a matter of life or death. Surely that is more important than their rules." She could hear the hysteria rising in her voice. This was everything she hated about India.

Ida's father patted her arm. "Now, now, there is nothing we can do about it. Our visitor is a deeply religious man, and we must respect his decision."

"Respect! I will never respect a man who lets his wife die. People here are crazy!" Ida snapped.

"Maybe so, but this is the way they have lived for thousands of years, and we can't change it overnight. It is best to forget about it."

"How can you say that?" Ida retorted. She had always thought of her father as a softhearted man, and now he was telling her to forget the fourteen-year-old girl dying in childbirth.

"Yes, forget," her father repeated. "It is a lesson that I learned a long time ago. There is so much suffering and despair here, and if I took it all to heart, I could not do my work. If there's nothing you can do to remedy a bad situation, the wisest thing to do is to forget about it."

"All right," Ida said impatiently, dissatisfied with her father's reply. "I was partway through writing a letter, and I want to finish it tonight." She turned and went back to her room.

When she sat down to write, Ida found her hand was shaking too much to hold the pen steady. Of course her father was right—she should forget about it. But how could she? She still recalled the starving children from when she was six years old. No wonder she hated India so much—it was full of horrible situations she could do nothing about.

Ida wiped a tear away with her sleeve and then smiled. What would Annie Hancock think of her getting so worked up over a woman she had never met! Ida decided she needed to pull herself together. With fresh resolve she picked up the pen and continued writing.

Ida had not even finished the page when she heard another noise outside her door. Her heart skipped a beat. Ida told herself the Brahman man had changed his mind. He had gone home, seen how desperate the situation was, and come back for her father's help.

Quickly Ida got up from her desk and flung open the door. "I am so glad you returned," she said before her eyes adjusted to the darkness.

A different voice spoke back to her. "Salaam, madam. May Allah grant you peace. I have come because I am in great need."

Ida peered at the man standing on the pathway. He was wearing a buttoned coat and a cap.

"Good evening," she replied. "What is it you need?"

The man stepped forward. "It is my wife," he said softly. "She has had other children, and they have been without trouble. But this one is different. She has been trying for a long time, but there is no one to help her except one woman who has no training. Forgive me for coming in the night, but I was hoping to find help. I hear you have a doctor here who has recently arrived from America."

"You mean my father," Ida replied. "Wait here and I will fetch him."

Without waiting for an answer, she ran off to find her father. This man was a Muslim, not a Brahman, and Ida saw no reason why his wife could not be seen by a male doctor. Even though one woman might die tonight, her father's expertise could surely save another.

A minute later Ida and her father stood facing the Muslim man. He was shaking his head vigorously.

"No, madam, you do not understand. Only a man of her immediate family can ever enter a Muslim woman's room," he said. "Forgive me, but is it not true that you are a doctor also?"

Ida could hardly believe it. What kind of cruel night was this? Two men from different religions, and both of them believed she was the only person who could save the lives of their wives.

"I can't help you. I don't know anything about medicine," she replied, and then she had an inspiration. "What if my father and I both came with you? He could look at your wife and tell me what to do, and I could do it. I would be the only one who touched her."

The Muslim man looked down. "No, if you cannot come, then it is the will of Allah that my wife die," he said in a flat voice, and with a bow he left.

This time Ida did not want to discuss the situation with her father. She knew what he would say— *If there's nothing you can do to remedy a bad situation, the wisest thing to do is to forget about it.* She did not want to hear that advice twice in one night. She fled back to her bedroom and locked the door behind her.

Ida wrote about what had happened and added:

> You can see now, Annie, why you wouldn't like to be a missionary, especially in India. You'd simply hate it. And I ought to know. Believe me, I'm going to get back home just as quickly as I possibly can. Why,

the people here don't even want you to help them. They'd rather let their wives and children die, even if they're beautiful and they say they love them and some of them are no more than fourteen.

Ida stopped for a moment. She heard a voice through the door. "Ammal, Ammal, are you there?"

Wearily Ida got up from her desk for the third time in an hour and opened the door. This time she knew the man who was standing there. He was Sri Mudaliar, the father of Kamla, one of her favorite pupils at the Hindu girls' school.

"Kamla? Is she all right? Has something bad happened?" she asked hurriedly.

"No," Sri Mudaliar said, speaking in broken English. "Kamla happy, but you must come to my house. Much trouble, very much trouble there."

Ida felt her throat tighten. She knew Kamla's mother was expecting a baby any day now. Surely it could not be another woman in labor! In a voice barely above a whisper, she asked, "Not your wife?"

"Yes, Ammal," Sri Mudaliar responded. "She is very sick. The baby is not arriving." Then, as Ida watched in horror, he knelt down in front of her and touched her feet with his hands. "Please, Missy Ammal. Please come, or my wife, she is dead."

"Get up off the ground. It will do no good for me to come. I don't know how to help your wife. My father can come. He is a doctor; he knows what to do." But even as she was saying the words, Ida knew it was useless. Sri Mudaliar would not allow a man to see his wife any more than the previous two husbands would.

"Missy, you come?" he pleaded hopefully.

"I would go with you if I could help you, but I can't. I don't know anything about medicine, and I would do her no good," Ida repeated, wishing that she was tucked up in bed and none of the events of this horrible night had happened.

"Sorry to bother, Missy," Sri Mudaliar said, bowing and walking backward at the same time. Before Ida could say anything else, he, too, was gone.

As the man disappeared into the dark, Ida asked herself what she could have said or done to change the situation. She could think of nothing.

Back in her bedroom, Ida decided to abandon her letter writing and go to bed so that no one else would see the lamp in her room. Maybe then she would get some peace.

Ten minutes later Ida was lying in bed. The only sounds she could hear were the swish of a tamarind branch against the roof and the occasional rustling of a lizard as it ran over the reed ceiling. But as much as Ida tried, she could not sleep. She could scarcely believe that three men, all with wives who were in the midst of difficult childbirths, had shown up on the veranda and all within the space of little more than an hour. And worse, all three men had rejected the offer of her father's help, preferring to sacrifice their wives' lives rather than break away from their religious beliefs.

For some reason the words of her father kept playing over and over in Ida's mind. *If there's nothing you can do to remedy a bad situation, the wisest thing to do is to forget about it.*

It was the word *if* that bothered Ida. Her father could not do anything about the situation regarding Hindu and Muslim women who needed medical attention because he was a man. But Ida was a woman, and there was something she could do to remedy the situation. But rather than give more thought to what she could do, Ida rolled over in bed and tried to think of other, more pleasant things. She planned out the dresses she would have made when she got back to the United States and the matching handbags and gloves she would buy. But it was no good. Her mind kept going back to the fact that she could do something about the situation if she wanted to.

It was a long night, and Ida did not sleep one moment of it. She worried about the women in labor, and the babies, and her own future. Eventually the sun came up and with it the sound of beating tom-toms. This was the sound Ida dreaded. It meant that someone in the village had died during the night.

Quickly Ida put on her slippers and dressing gown and slipped out of her room into the courtyard of the mission house. Souri, one of the servants, was just arriving for work, and Ida called to him.

"Souri, do you know who died last night?" she asked.

"No, Missy Ida, I do not," he replied.

"I want you to find out for me. It is very important."

"Yes, Missy," Souri replied. "Right away I shall go."

Ida sat on the veranda steps waiting impatiently for Souri to return. The sun rose in golden splendor over the trees, but she hardly noticed it. Eventually she saw Souri's yellow hat bobbing above the stone wall that surrounded the mission compound. When Souri opened the gate, Ida noticed how grim he looked.

"Did you find out?" she asked. "Please tell me."

"It is not good news," Souri replied. "Three women died in the night, and each of them with a newborn child."

"I see," Ida said, not trusting herself to say any more.

Right about then the first funeral procession began winding its way along the street the mission compound was located on as people made their way to the burning grounds by the river. Ida fled back into her bedroom at the sight of the procession.

Ida stayed in her bedroom for a long time, sitting on the bed thinking about all the things that as late as yesterday had seemed important to her. Now they seemed silly and useless. What was the point of spending her time deciding between a satin skirt and a velvet dress? Or between a lace bonnet and a glittering hair clasp. Was that what she was going back to America for? Was she going back to live a life full of trivial moments? Suddenly Ida heard herself praying aloud, "God, if You want me to, I will spend the rest of my life in India trying to help these women."

There, she had said it. And instead of feeling like she had just thrown her life away, Ida felt invigorated! She flung her clothes on and rushed out the door. A minute later she was standing in the dispensary facing her father. Ida smiled as she spoke. "This morning I have come to a decision," she began. "Father, last night when those men came, you said, 'If there's nothing you can do to remedy a bad situation, the wisest thing to do is to forget about it.' Well, I couldn't forget about those women, *and there is something I can do about it.* As soon as Mother is completely well, I am going back to the United States to study medicine, and then I am coming back to India to help the women and babies."

Chapter 6

Dr. Ida Sophia Scudder

Ida would have liked to jump on the first ship bound for the United States and begin her medical studies, but her mother was not yet well enough to assume all her responsibilities. Ida's parents urged their daughter to stay with them for a while longer instead of returning to America right away. Ida agreed to do so and helped out wherever she could. But now she had a real interest in the people around her. She worked hard to learn the intricacies of the language and better understand the culture around her.

In 1892, about the time Ida hoped to be free to return to the United States, Uncle Jared, his wife, and his daughter Dixie went back to the United States for a two-year furlough. This created a crisis.

There was no one to run the medical mission at Vellore. Eventually it was decided that Ida and her parents should move there, leaving Henry to run the work at Tindivanam. In Vellore Ida would manage the daily running of the mission station while her father traveled between there and Tindivanam carrying on his medical work.

Ida was happy enough to move to Vellore, though she did wish she were going home and not Dixie. How ironic it seemed to Ida that just a year ago she had been the one bursting to leave India while Dixie wanted to stay forever in some forgotten little village. Now Dixie was on her way to the United States and Ida was staying behind in India to take over her responsibilities.

The town of Vellore was a pleasant place to live. It had about forty thousand people, and since it was the center for the British colonial government for the North Arcot district, there were many English people among its population. There was even a British judge and police superintendent and an English club where British citizens could play polo, croquet, and card games. Although none of these things interested Ida, she liked to go the club to speak English and catch up on the latest world news.

Vellore, which was much cleaner than Tindivanam, sat in a valley surrounded by rocky hills. Whenever she could, Ida would walk up into the hills, breathing in the fresh, crisp air. Her cousin, Dr. Lew Scudder, worked at Ranipet, just ten miles away, and sometimes Ida walked there to see him.

Within a month Ida found herself slipping into Dixie's shoes. Dixie had run two schools for Hindu girls, with a combined enrollment of two hundred girls. Ida loved working with the girls. However, in September 1892 the enrollment plummeted. It all started when Lakshmi, one of the brightest Brahman students, did not return to school after a lunch break. Ida was a little concerned about this, and she sent a servant around to find out what the problem was. The servant soon returned with the news that Lakshmi was not at home and that her parents had not seen her since that morning.

More inquiries were made, but no one had heard or seen anything of the ten-year-old. Ida hoped that she had just wandered off on her own for a while, but deep down she knew that was unlikely. Lakshmi loved to come to school.

The night passed, and still there was no word of Lakshmi. Another day and night passed, and Ida became frantic trying to imagine what could have happened. Lakshmi's parents, while they did not know what had happened to her, certainly had suspicions as to why something terrible had befallen their daughter. They believed it was because they had committed two great sins. First, they had allowed their daughter to acquire knowledge when that was a man's role, and second, and worse, they had allowed her to go to a Christian school. They told Ida it was no wonder the gods were punishing them.

Soon the entire town knew why Lakshmi's parents thought she was missing, and one by one the

Hindu girls stopped coming to school. Their parents feared that they, too, might disappear without a trace.

A month after Lakshmi's disappearance, Ida learned that her parents had received a postcard informing them that their daughter's body was at the bottom of a well on the north side of town. Sure enough, that is where the body was found. The police superintendent investigated the murder, and it turned out that four men had been looking for buried treasure. They were unable to locate any, and so they offered up Lakshmi (who was named after the goddess of prosperity) as a human sacrifice to the goddess in the hope that she would tell them where treasure was hidden.

The murder and the reason for it sickened Ida. She was furious that the men had not only killed one of her best students but also frightened many other promising girls out of the opportunity of receiving an education.

The next two years sped by as Ida continued her work. Before long Uncle Jared, his wife, and Dixie returned to Vellore. By now it was time for Ida's parents to take a furlough, and so arrangements were made for the three of them to sail back to the United States together in the fall of 1894. Ida's brother Henry accompanied them. He had decided to return to the United States and study to become an ordained minister, after which he hoped to again return to India.

When they set sail on the journey to America, Ida could hardly believe she had been in India for four years.

As the journey progressed, Ida often sat on deck. The ship rocked gently beneath her as she considered how she was going to pay for her education. From talks with her cousin Lew, she knew that medical school would cost about $150 a year. But all the money Ida had amounted to about $10, and she knew her parents did not have much more.

It was wonderful to be home again when the ship finally docked in New York. Ida's parents set up house in New Brunswick, New Jersey, where brothers Charles and Walter then joined Henry and Ida. Soon the three brothers all set about earning theology degrees, but it took Ida a little longer to start her career.

In June the following year, Ida found herself in front of the Women's Auxiliary Board of the Reformed Church. The board was debating whether it was appropriate to send a single female doctor to work in India. The debate seemed endless. Despite Ida's description of the unforgettable night when three women died because there was no female doctor to treat them, many women on the auxiliary board were concerned. Only fifty years had passed since Elizabeth Blackwell had become the first woman doctor in the United States, and many people were still not comfortable with the idea of a woman doing a "man's" job.

Eventually one of the younger women, Kate Ferlinghuysen, stood up. "Enough of this," she said. "If Ida Scudder feels called to work in India, then I move that we give her an education and send her there." With that she unclipped her purse and pulled out a banknote. "And here," she said waving the bill, "is the first ten dollars."

Other women nodded in agreement, and soon a resolution was passed allowing the mission to sponsor Ida through medical school. Ida planned to attend the Women's Medical College of Philadelphia, one of only a handful of accredited colleges that accepted women, and one of the best. The top medical schools, like Cornell, did not accept any women into their programs.

Ida started on her degree in the spring of 1896. It was a four-year course, and she was eager to get working, as she would be at least thirty before she saw India again.

Medical school did not prove easy for Ida. She soon found that her education at Northfield Seminary had not provided a good foundation for medical school, not to mention the fact that she had forgotten much of what she had learned there, anyway. Undeterred, Ida joined a sorority, and the women studied together and encouraged each other along. One by one she passed her courses, gaining confidence as she went.

As 1897 began to draw to a close, Ida's parents felt well rested and ready to return to their posts in India. By now Henry had finished his studies and married a local New Brunswick girl named Margaret Booraem, and the young couple was going to accompany Dr. and Mrs. Scudder back to India.

Christmas 1897 represented the last chance for the Scudder family to be together for at least four years. Everyone made the effort to meet at a summer cottage on Shelter Island in Long Island Sound. Ida was overjoyed to see everyone again. Her brother John and his wife and children came by train from California, and Lewis and his family traveled from Nebraska, where they still lived on the farm.

It turned out to be a Christmas to remember. Despite the cold water, Ida and her brothers swam every day, with Ida covering a mile before breakfast. There were clambakes and yacht races, tennis matches, and hikes across the island. But for Ida it all ended too quickly, and it was soon time to say goodbye to her father, mother, and brothers.

When Ida returned to Philadelphia, surprising news awaited that took her mind off her family. Cornell Medical College, one of the most prestigious colleges in America, had been given an endowment of one and a half million dollars, on one condition— that the school accept women students!

Everyone at the Women's Medical College of Philadelphia was soon asking the same question: if Cornell opened to women, who among them would be brave enough to be in the first graduating class?

It did not take Ida long to decide she wanted to transfer to Cornell. Cornell Medical College was located in New York City, and there were much better clinical opportunities in New York. Ida also hoped that there would be more emphasis on tropical diseases there.

When Cornell finally opened its doors to women, Ida and her roommate, Nell Bartholomew, rode their bicycles to New York City to transfer for their final year of school. This meant a lot of extra work for Ida and Nell, as they both had to complete the first three years of clinical labs as well as keep up with all the normal final-year requirements.

At first it was difficult for Ida to concentrate on her studies. Only a handful of women were at Cornell, and the male students whistled and stamped their feet whenever they came into a room. However, after a while the men tired of such taunting, and things calmed down.

Although there was not as much emphasis on tropical diseases as Ida would have liked, her father's weekly letters kept her up-to-date on what was happening in India. Cholera had reached epidemic proportions in southern India, and hundreds of Ida's father's patients were dying every week. Many weird rumors were spread about how the disease started. One of these rumors was that a touch from a Western doctor was all it took to catch the disease. As a result, for several months, Dr. Scudder had sticks and stones thrown at him whenever he left the mission compound. Despite this, he wrote to Ida and told her of an ambitious program he dreamed of—to inoculate the local people against cholera. It was a procedure that had been known for only a few months.

Ida's father was convinced that inoculation would save thousands of lives, and so he arranged for the government surgeon to pay a visit to Vellore. He then gathered all the local Christians together and explained to them how the inoculation worked.

Wanting to be sure they understood how simple it was, Dr. Scudder rolled up his own sleeve and was the first person in South India to be inoculated against cholera. Many brave Christians followed his example. Within weeks the next wave of cholera spread through the region. However, because they had been inoculated, the Christians did not catch the disease. Suddenly Dr. Scudder was mobbed wherever he went—not by hostile crowds but by people wanting the inoculation themselves.

Ida was glad to read about this. The approach of the turn of the twentieth century was proving to be a time of great medical breakthroughs, and she wanted to learn as much about them all as she could.

In the middle of the year, Ida had the opportunity to say hello, and goodbye, to Dr. Louisa Hart. Dr. Hart was a young Canadian woman who had been recruited by Ida's cousin in Ranipet, Dr. Lew Scudder. She had traveled to New York to catch a ship to India. Meeting Louisa Hart made Ida even more anxious to return to India herself. Perhaps, she hoped, they might be able to work together sometime soon.

To add more excitement, Ida's brother Walter had fallen in love with Ida's roommate, Nell, and the two of them announced their engagement. The couple intended to go to India after their wedding, making three female doctors who planned to serve there. Ida could hardly believe how blessed she was to have her best friend marry her brother. And as if that were not enough, Annie Hancock, Ida's friend from Northfield Seminary, had applied to the mission board to go with Ida to India.

The final year of medical college continued, and Ida was so busy she hardly had time to think. She spent her clinical assignment delivering babies in the slums on the Lower East Side. Then, finally, in June 1899 it was all over. Ida had taken her last exam, and now all she had to do was wait for the results. She hoped and prayed she had passed.

In the meantime she moved out of the college dorm and into a house on Fifty-sixth Street that was owned by an elderly spinster, Katharine Van Nest, the Women's Auxiliary secretary for India. Ida planned to stay with Katharine until November, when she planned to sail back to India, hopefully with Annie Hancock.

Much to her relief, Ida learned in July that she had passed her exams. She was now Dr. Ida Sophia Scudder.

Now that Ida was a doctor, the mission directors had a new assignment to keep her busy until she sailed for India. It was an assignment that both surprised and delighted her. In the short time Dr. Louisa Hart had been in Ranipet, she had seen for herself the terrible situation the women of India found themselves in, and she had come to her own conclusion: there should be a hospital for women in Vellore. The mission agreed, and now it was Ida's job to raise the eight thousand dollars necessary to build and supply the hospital.

Eight thousand dollars! Ida gulped at the huge amount that needed to be raised. But at the same time, she was thrilled by the whole idea of raising the money. With three female doctors and an assistant like Annie Hancock, her mind buzzed with the things that could be done through the hospital.

Ida set to work right away, making lists of people to call on and drawing up charts of facts and figures. She found that in India there was one doctor for every ninety-five hundred people, whereas in the United States there was one doctor for every five hundred people. No wonder, she concluded, that the life expectancy for Indians was twenty-six years while life expectancy for Americans was fifty-four years. India desperately needed more hospitals and more doctors to staff them, and especially a hospital for women.

Ida found few people who were interested in hearing about plans to build a hospital for women in far-off India, and fewer still who were willing to make a donation toward it. With just ten days left before she was due to set sail for India, she had only a few hundred dollars in hand that she had collected, not nearly enough to make a start on the project.

Still, Ida would not give up. She felt sure that God meant for them to have a hospital for women and that the money would come, somehow. On Saturday night, a week before she was to leave, Ida sat alone in the front room. Katharine came in carrying two cups of coffee.

"You look like you need some cheering up," Katharine said, handing Ida a cup.

"I do," Ida admitted. "It's so frustrating. I have given my presentation a hundred times, but no one seems to care. Is there something wrong with it? Aren't I putting things the right way? I just wish I could take people to India and show them, let them see the misery and need."

"I know, I know," Katharine replied, patting Ida's leg. "Sometimes God has strange ways of doing things. You mustn't give up." She walked over to her desk and picked up a piece of paper. "In fact," she continued, "I have an idea. I received this church bulletin in the mail today from the Collegiate Church down the street. They are having a missionary society meeting this Monday morning. Perhaps you could speak to them all. I know their president well. Her name is Miss Taber, and she lives a block from here."

Before Ida could say anything, Katharine had picked up a pen and started writing. "In fact, my dear, I will write you a note of introduction right now, and you can pay her a visit this evening."

Ida ran upstairs to freshen up and returned to find Katharine waiting with her hat and shawl. "I'll be praying while you're gone," she said with a twinkle in her eye.

As she hurried down Fifty-sixth Street, Ida hoped for the best. Surely God was going to answer her prayers for a hospital that night. She stopped at the right address and rang the doorbell. A maid answered, and Ida handed her the letter of introduction. Soon an elderly woman appeared at the door.

"I'm Miss Taber," the woman said, holding out her hand. "Please come in and tell me what it is you want."

Ida was led through the hallway into a sitting room, where an old man was reading a newspaper. The man barely looked up as Miss Taber said, "This is my brother-in-law, Mr. Robert Schell. I am sure he will excuse us."

With that she walked on into the adjoining library and asked the maid to bring them tea. Once they were settled into matching leather armchairs, Ida told Miss Taber all about the plans for the hospital in Vellore. She described the terrible night when the three women had died, and the joy it would be to save mothers and their babies. She described how her father operated on men and boys out in the open, with nothing but a sheet for an operating table.

When she was finished, Miss Taber smiled. "Well, dear," she said, "you certainly have a passion for your cause, but I'm afraid to tell you that the Collegiate Church already sponsors many missionary projects." She shook her head, and Ida had to fight to keep the tears from welling up in her eyes.

Miss Taber continued. "However, I see no harm in your presenting the need for a hospital to the Mission Society meeting on Monday morning. How about meeting me there at 9:15. You never know; they might vote to give you several hundred dollars."

As Ida thanked Miss Taber for her time and got up to leave, she felt like a balloon that had just been pricked. She stumbled past Mr. Schell and out the door into the fresh air. Instead of going directly back to the house, Ida walked blocks out of her way. She needed time to calm down. But no matter how fast she walked, she could not stop thinking about the words "they might vote to give you several hundred dollars." Several hundred dollars was a drop in the bucket compared to the needs of Indian women. Ida had been sure that the visit to Miss Taber was the answer to her problems raising money for the hospital, but it turned out to be just the same as so many other visits—a promise to listen and not much more. Ida wondered whether she should return to India without the money or stay behind in the United States and keep trying to raise it. She prayed about what to do, but no answer came.

Chapter 7

Provision

Ida arrived at breakfast the next morning still not knowing what she should do. She had just finished buttering a piece of toast for herself when the maid came in with a note on a tray.

"For you, Dr. Scudder," she said.

Ida took the note and opened it. The handwriting was a little shaky, but the message was unmistakable. "Please visit me at your earliest convenience tomorrow morning at my sister-in-law's house." The note was signed "Robert Schell."

Ida read the note out loud to Katharine.

"You didn't tell me that you met with Miss Taber's brother-in-law," Katharine said.

"Well, I didn't really," Ida responded, puzzling over what the old man could want. "I just said hello to him as I walked through the room. He was read-ing the newspaper, and he hardly looked up."

"But he wants to see you. Do you know what that could mean?" Katharine asked.

"No," Ida stammered.

"Mr. Schell is the president of the Bank of the Metropolis in New York. Of course, he is very wealthy. Perhaps he is interested in your work, Ida!"

"But I didn't even tell him about it."

Katharine laughed. "Dear, there is only one way to find out what he wants, and that's to put on your hat and coat after breakfast tomorrow and pay him a visit."

Ida nervously ate her toast and boiled egg. What was it the old man wanted?

Ida was nervous all day long, and then at eight o'clock the following morning, she walked back to Miss Taber's house. Soon she was being escorted to the same room she had been in two days before. Only this time Robert Schell was seated behind a desk, glasses perched on the end of his nose doing some figuring. He looked up as Ida entered the room.

"Come in. Please sit down," Mr. Schell said. "I must confess I overheard your conversation with my sister-in-law the day before yesterday, and I have a few questions I want to ask you."

Ida nodded, and Mr. Schell opened a notebook on the desk. He started down a list of questions that covered everything from what buildings were con-structed of in Vellore to whether a railway station served the town to what Ida's qualifications were.

Of course Ida admitted that she presently did not have the qualifications to run the hospital, but she assured Mr. Schell that her father would be at her side until she learned enough about medical conditions in India to do it herself. She anticipated this would take about four years.

Finally Mr. Schell ran out of questions to ask. He leaned forward in his chair and picked up a pen. "You have answered my questions well," he said. "For some time I have been looking for a suitable way to honor my wife's memory, and I think I have found it. While she was alive, she took a great interest in missions and particularly in the welfare of women in foreign lands." His voice choked as he spoke. He then abruptly reached for a checkbook and wrote out a check. "Here," he said. "I know you were asking for eight thousand dollars to get the hospital up and running, but I have decided to give you ten thousand dollars. I want this hospital to be worthy of my wife's memory."

Ida's hands trembled as she reached for the check. It was overwhelming to think that the piece of paper she held in her hand represented enough money to buy a whole hospital! As she thanked Mr. Schell, she wondered how many lives would be saved as a result of his generosity.

"One more thing," Mr. Schell said. "I suppose you will be importing the equipment you need from the United States, is that right?"

"Yes," Ida replied. "There is very little equipment available in India."

"That's what I thought," Mr. Schell said. "It's no use having a hospital without equipment, is it? How about we go to a medical supply store together, and you can pick out what you need. I'll write a check to cover the cost of it. I believe you have a meeting at my sister-in-law's church at ten o'clock, so I will pick you up there at 12:30, and we will go shopping. How would that be?"

"Wonderful," Ida replied. "Simply wonderful."

An hour later Ida found herself standing in front of the Missionary Society of the Collegiate Church. Instead of asking for money to build the hospital, she was able to tell the women that the money had been supplied. However, Ida took the opportunity to tell those in attendance about the need for staff for the hospital and how her friend Annie Hancock was looking for people to sponsor her so that she could go and work alongside Ida.

When Ida was finished, the mission secretary thanked her for her presentation and promised that the group would consider helping Annie in some modest way, if and when they had some extra money.

Ida was not terribly disappointed by this response; she was still so excited that the hospital and equipment were all paid for. But when the meeting was over, a small group of women clustered around Ida, wanting to know more about her work in Vellore. One petite woman with piercing black eyes caught Ida's attention.

"I am Gertrude Dodd," the woman said quietly. "My two sisters are here with me, and we have been discussing your situation. We think it is such a pity that your friend is ready and willing to go to India and no one will send her, so we have decided to take care of her expenses. You tell your friend she is going with you to India."

Ida felt her eyes misting over. "I can't tell you... how much...how much this means to me," she sputtered.

"You don't have to," Gertrude replied, patting Ida's arm. "I can see how much you care for those Indian women. And I am sure your friend will be a great help to you."

Ida was still in a state of shock when Robert Schell's carriage rolled up and a coachman swept open the door for her. She felt like a princess as the horses pulled her along Fifth Avenue to the medical supply store, where Mr. Schell insisted she select all of the fittings and instruments she could possibly want for the hospital. Then he asked for it all to be crated up so that it could sail on the same ship as Ida.

The ship, with Ida and Annie aboard, sailed from New York for Madras on Monday, November 22, 1899. The voyage was expected to take seven weeks, but with favorable winds and currents, it took only six. During the voyage Ida celebrated her twenty-ninth birthday.

On the first day of the new year, January 1, 1900, Ida Scudder finally set foot back in India. To Ida it seemed like a wonderful day to start her new life as a doctor in India. By that evening Ida was back in

Vellore with her parents, who were thrilled to see her and Annie. Ida's parents had gotten to know Annie while they were in the United States on furlough.

Even though Ida was tired from the trip, she was alert enough to notice that her father was slower than she remembered him. When she was alone with her mother, she asked about her father. Her mother told her that he had not been the same since he inoculated himself against cholera. Ida thought that the inoculation might have been too strong, but all she could do was watch over her father and hope that he got healthy again.

Ida tried to work alongside her father, but it was not easy. Nobody appeared to trust her. No matter how small their problem, the men who came to the clinic all wanted her father to treat them, and no women sought out her services either.

In the meantime Annie fit right in to the work at Vellore. She starting visiting the homes in town that were hospitable to missionaries, and she made friends with many of the women. Ida reminded Annie to tell the women that there was a female doctor who could treat them now, and she prayed that someone would ask for her services soon. After all, if she could not attract one female patient, what was the point of building an entire hospital for them?

Finally, three weeks after her arrival back in India, a young boy tugged on Ida's sleeve. "Missy Doctor Ammal?" he asked.

"Yes," Ida replied in Tamil, "I am a doctor."

"The old woman at my house is very sick. Will you come?"

That was just the question Ida wanted to hear. In one movement she scooped up her medical bag and headed for the door. She had the stable boy harness the pony and carriage in record time, and she beckoned the young boy to climb on board with her. Not waiting for a servant to drive them, Ida took the reins and urged the pony out the gate and on down the street.

The pony trotted through the dusty streets toward the bazaar. As they made their way, the boy pointed to Fort Hill Street and then jumped off the carriage. Ida drew the carriage to a sudden halt and jumped off after the boy.

"Why are you leaving me?" Ida asked.

It took a minute or two for her to understand, but with a combination of gestures and Tamil she learned that the boy belonged to a low caste and could not go down that particular street to the house because many people of high caste lived on the street. He would have to go the long way around.

Ida was so frustrated with the whole caste system that she wanted to lecture the boy on how ridiculous it all was, but she remembered her errand and left it at that. She turned the carriage onto Fort Hill Street and, following the boy's instructions, was able to locate a house with a carved doorway and three pillars. The door swung open on a woman who cowered in the dimly lit room. The woman beckoned, and Ida followed her down a passageway, through a courtyard, and into another dark room.

Ida squinted to adjust to the darkness, annoyed at the Indian custom of keeping sick people in a dark, airless environment. Then Ida heard a moan from the corner and noticed the outline of a woman lying on a mat. She hurried over to the woman, knelt down, and felt her forehead. It was cold. She reached for the woman's wrist and held it a long time trying to locate a pulse. Eventually she felt a faint rhythm.

O God, what should I do? Ida prayed to herself. She knew that the woman, her first patient, was near death. The woman was beyond help, but if Ida stayed with her till she died, word would get around that she could not save the woman. She debated whether to stay or go. But who was going to make this pitiful woman comfortable in her dying hour? Ida realized she had to stay and make the best of the situation.

She called for the man of the house and explained to him that there was nothing she could do to save this woman's life, but if he would let her, she would stay and make her comfortable. Ida knew of the local custom that did not allow a sick person to have water or fresh air, and she wanted the woman to have both.

Much to Ida's surprise, the man summoned the old woman's three daughters-in-law from some-where deep within the house and told them to do whatever Missy Ammal told them to. This was all Ida needed to hear. She ordered the younger women to carry their mother-in-law out of the sti-fling room and into a shaded part of the courtyard. Then she asked for water, which was brought to her. Ida dripped some of the cool liquid into the old woman's mouth and then wet her handkerchief and sponged her off.

While Ida was doing this, the old woman lay with her eyes wide open, following Ida's every move. Ida continued to dip her handkerchief in water and sponge the old woman as the minutes turned into hours. Finally Ida needed to stretch herself. As she stood up, the old woman pulled on her dress. Ida looked down to see the woman roll onto her stomach and edge her way down the mat until she was level with Ida's feet. Then, in a supreme effort, the old woman lifted her face and kissed Ida's feet. Ida jumped back.

"No, no!" she exclaimed. Then she knelt down again and looked into the old woman's eyes. There was a sign of recognition, and then nothing. The act of rising to kiss Ida's feet had been the woman's last act.

The three younger women crowded around Ida as she shut the old woman's eyes and placed the handkerchief gently over her face.

Quietly Ida stood up and walked across the courtyard toward the main door. The women crowded in around her.

"You come back and see us. Please. Please. You are our friend. Don't forget you are our friend," they said.

Ida looked at them. "I will come back and see you," she promised, confident that she had indeed made her first real friends in Vellore.

Chapter 8

The Mary Taber Schell
Memorial Hospital

Ida and her father were bicycling quietly along the path that led back to the Reformed Church's missionary guest house in Kodaikanal, a popular resort town in the hills above Madras. It was May, and Ida was glad for a break from the sweltering heat of the plains below. She knew she needed a rest, and her father needed one even more. Ida was concerned about his health. In some ways he did seem better, but he was plagued with large boils that left him weak and sore.

The two of them had just turned a corner when Mr. Scudder's front wheel bumped against a tree root. In an instant Ida's father shot over the handlebars and onto the path. Ida jumped off her bicycle and ran to his aid. She took his hands to help him up, but he could not summon the strength to get to his feet.

"Just lie there," Ida said. "You don't need to move. Someone will be along to help us in a minute."

Ida ran her hands over her father's legs and arms, but she could not feel any broken bones. She examined his head, but he had not hit it when he fell.

"I am sorry to spoil your fun," her father said as he lay on the ground.

Within a minute or two, a group of young men came riding along, and they rushed to help. Between them they made a makeshift stretcher and carried John Scudder back to the guest house.

Mrs. Scudder ran out to see what all the commotion was about. With her usual efficiency, she cleared the furniture out of the way so that her husband could be laid on his bed.

Ida's cousin, Dr. Lew Scudder, who was also staying at the house, grabbed his medical bag and asked everyone except Ida to leave the room. Ida shut the door gently just as her cousin was taking off her father's shirt. Ida and Lew both let out a gasp at the same moment. John Scudder had lumps as large as golf balls under both arms.

"Why didn't you tell us?" Ida exclaimed.

"I didn't want to be a bother," her father responded, "what with you starting out in your work. You have plenty more important things to worry about. It's probably nothing serious."

Ida and Lew looked at each other. Even though Ida was a new doctor, she was convinced she was looking at a very serious condition—cancer—and she was sure her father knew it too.

Together the two cousins made Dr. Scudder comfortable, and then Lew signaled for Ida to meet him outside.

"We must operate now," Lew said as soon as the two of them were out of the elder doctor's hearing.

"But we can't," Ida replied. "The nearest hospital is in Madura. He would never survive the trip there."

"Then we'll do it here," Lew replied. "It's the only chance he has."

Ida felt her mouth go dry. "Do you think so?" she asked. "Is it that serious?"

Ida's cousin did not say a word but just nodded his head.

The next five days were agony for Ida as she waited for the correct operating equipment to be sent from the nearest hospital. The operation was scheduled for noon, when the best light was available, and the veranda was prepared as an operating room.

Ida grew more nervous as the time for the operation approached. Lew was going to do the operating while Ida and her brother Walter and sister-in-law Nell took charge of sterilizing the equipment and handing it to Lew.

Finally noon came, and all of the sheets and dressings had been boiled and dried over the woodstove. Lew, Ida, Walter, and Nell all put on operating gowns, and Lew held a chloroform cloth over John's nose, rendering him unconscious.

Ida's medical training helped her focus, and she automatically did what her cousin asked, handing him a scalpel and other instruments and holding out a pan for him to place the cancerous growths in.

"It's not good," Lew said after operating on Ida's father's right armpit. "The growth is large, and I don't think I can get it all."

Still, the four of them labored on together. Sadly, Lew was even less optimistic about removing the growth in the other armpit. He removed what he could and quickly sewed up the incision.

"All we can do is wait and pray," he said as he snipped the last suture.

Ida stood by numbly watching her father. Was it possible that he was really dying? The idea seemed outrageous to her, like some nightmare from which she would soon awaken.

After a few moments Ida's father stirred. He opened his eyes. "O, Master, let the light go out," he murmured and then lapsed into unconsciousness.

They were the last words he ever spoke. He lay quietly for a few more hours and then stopped breathing.

The entire town of Kodaikanal was shocked. It seemed impossible that they had lost their beloved Dr. Scudder, but no one was more devastated than Ida. Her father was her mentor, the man who was showing her the way to treat tropical diseases and relate to the Indian people. And she had worked with him for only five months. It didn't seem fair. How could she go on without him?

The next day Dr. John Scudder II was buried in the Kodaikanal cemetery. Ida barely heard the many eulogies that were spoken at the service; she was lost in her grief, stunned at how quickly her father had died.

The following weeks passed in a haze. Somehow Ida and her mother returned to Vellore, though Ida could not bear to open her father's clinic. She missed him too much. Besides, she knew she did not have the medical experience she needed to work alone.

As the days rolled by, Ida began to imagine a modest clinic for herself. She and Annie opened one of the front rooms in the house and spread the word that Ida would see patients there until the hospital was opened in a few months, when Dr. Louisa Hart would move to Vellore to run it.

On the first morning the clinic was open, Ida had everything ready by eight o'clock. The house girl, Salomi, had neatly lined up the medicines on shelves, bandages were rolled, and Ida's medical tools were laid out on a white sheet on the table. Ida waited until noon, but no one came. Nor did anyone come the following day or the day after that. In fact, two weeks went by, and not a single patient showed up at the clinic. Ida double-checked with the butler and the stable hand to make sure they had spread the word that things were "back to normal" at the mission house. But in reality they were not. There was no male doctor there anymore, and no one appeared to want to be Ida's first patient.

Ida was so frustrated with the situation that she cried herself to sleep many nights during this time. She wondered what use a hospital in Vellore would be if her father was not there to run it. It seemed that women doctors could not inspire confidence in a land like India.

A break finally came when a bandy pulled up in the driveway. From the back of the cart stepped a woman clad in an expensive silk sari. Her eyes were bandaged, and a young girl led her by the hand up the steps of the clinic.

Ida's heart jumped. "Please, God," she prayed, "let this be something simple that I can cure."

With more confidence than she felt, Ida welcomed the woman into the clinic and unwrapped the bandages. The woman's eyes were red and weeping with yellow pus.

"Thank you, God," Ida said as she poured some boric solution from a bottle to bathe the woman's eyes. "You have conjunctivitis. I am going to put some drops in your eyes, and you will need to return every morning for a week for more drops. Then you will be cured. Do you understand?" she said to the woman.

The woman repeated the instructions back to Ida and then left.

Once the woman was gone, Ida realized that in her excitement at finally having a patient, she had forgotten to ask the woman her name or address. Now she had no way of following up if the woman did not return to the clinic. The next morning, however, the woman did show up, and she brought with her another woman with the same eye problem.

By the end of the week, both women were better, and other patients, both men and women, began to come to the clinic. Before long Ida was very busy, so busy, in fact, that she began praying for a Tamil-speaking assistant. Annie did what she could to help, but by now she was occupied visiting the local women in their homes.

As it turned out, the answer to Ida's prayer was right in front of her. Ida had noticed that the house girl, Salomi Benjamin, was finding excuses to spend time around the clinic and that she had picked up a lot of information about medicines from watching Ida dispense them. Unlike most Indian girls, Salomi could read and write Tamil and speak English. Ida approached her about working full-time in the clinic. Salomi's eyes sparkled with delight at the idea, and soon she and Ida were an inseparable team.

In the meantime the new forty-bed hospital was slowly emerging from the red dust of Vellore. Named the Mary Taber Schell Memorial Hospital after Robert Schell's wife, the cornerstone for the structure was laid on September 7, 1901. One year later the building was opened with great pomp and ceremony.

At the opening, crowds of people clamored to see the strange white wrought-iron beds with wire-spring bases and thick mattresses. They had never seen anything like it before. Nor had they ever seen anything like the shiny operating room, complete with autoclave and glass-topped table.

The hospital was divided into two parts. The first, a large open ward, was for poor patients who could not afford to pay for their stay. The second part of the hospital was for patients from higher castes who could not mix with the poor lower-caste patients or even eat food from the kitchen that served the rest of the hospital. The rooms for high-caste patients had their own cooking stoves so that a family member could prepare food for the patient.

Within days of opening, the hospital began to fill up with sick and dying patients. Unfortunately, Dr. Louisa Hart, the woman who had suggested the hospital in the first place, was not there to help Ida. She had become sick and had returned to the United States to recuperate. This was a blow to Ida, who still desperately missed her father and had been counting on Louisa to run the hospital.

Adding to the challenge, when the Schell Hospital opened, South India was in the grip of a famine brought on by the failure of the monsoon rains. Ida soon found herself overwhelmed with starving and diseased people. Some of them had walked a hundred miles in the hope of being fed. Just as had been done when Ida was a small child, feeding stations were set up at the mission, and everywhere Ida went, people begged her for food and water. Throughout this time Salomi was always at Ida's side, helping in any way she could.

Some cases Ida simply did not feel experienced enough to handle without the support of an older doctor. One of these cases presented itself soon after the hospital opened. A young girl was admitted who had a huge tumor in her stomach. Ida froze with fright when she saw it. Up until now she had delivered babies, lanced abscesses, and carried out other simple procedures, but she had never undertaken a major operation on her own. She trembled as she stood on the veranda and told her mother about it.

"I just can't do it. It's not that I don't want to help her, but cutting into someone's stomach is a major operation, and I am not ready for it," she confided.

"Do you know anyone around here who is more ready than you?" her mother asked.

"No," Ida stammered, "but you don't understand. If I do something wrong, she could die on the operating table."

"And if you don't do anything, won't she die anyway? Suppose she died because there was no woman doctor who had the courage to operate on her. Wouldn't that be the worst case of all?" Mrs. Scudder asked.

"Yes," Ida replied, as a look of understanding spread across her face.

She turned and walked away with determination in her step. She was ready to operate, and she needed to do it quickly before she lost her resolve. She called Salomi to bring the patient to the operating room as she made preparations for the operation. Before she picked up the scalpel, she prayed, asking God to guide her hands and keep them steady.

Thankfully, things went well with the operation, and the girl made a complete recovery. Ida was relieved and felt encouraged to continue treating the most difficult cases admitted to the hospital.

Some patients, however, Ida could not treat because their families forbade it. These cases were the most depressing of all for her to deal with. One woman needed an immediate operation or she would die. The woman, who had five small children at home, desperately wanted Ida to operate on her, but her husband refused to allow it. Ida could do nothing as the woman was lifted onto a bandy and taken home to die. Ida knew that she was fighting ignorance and superstition every bit as much as she was fighting poor hygiene and disease.

Finally, late in 1902, rain began to fall and the drought was broken. By the time crops were growing in the fields and the famine subsided, it had been a tough first year for the new hospital and its lone doctor. Ida had treated over twelve thousand patients and performed 56 major and 428 minor operations.

Tragically, the famine was followed by bubonic plague, which swept through Vellore in 1903. Many people were already weak from more than a year with little food, and Ida watched as about twenty patients a day perished from the plague. Although a vaccine was available, many people refused to take it. Rumors spread that European doctors were using the vaccine to murder Indian people and that the British Empire was paying them a good sum of money each time they succeeded.

Such rumors made things difficult for Ida, and before long not a single patient was willing to brave the hospital. Instead Ida took her skills into the town, where she was sometimes invited into a home to treat an ailing person. But normally, by the time she arrived, it was too late to do much except make the patient comfortable and urge the rest of the family to get inoculated.

In the four weeks that the bubonic plague raged in and around Vellore, a total of four hundred people died. And by the time the plague abated throughout southern India, it had taken the lives of over one million people.

Once the plague passed, patients returned to the hospital, and several new helpers joined the staff. One of these was a pharmacist named Mrs. Gnanammal, a thirty-five-year-old Christian widow. She was very efficient, and Ida was soon relying on her to mix the medicines for the hospital and train Salomi. Another Indian woman, Guanasundram, joined the staff, along with Mary Henry, a nearly blind woman whom Ida made hospital matron. Ida's mother also helped. With these capable women at her side, Ida began to share the burden of running the hospital.

At times Ida felt an uncanny urge to double-check on a patient. One of these occasions occurred in September 1903. Ida was sitting in her dispensary, ready to examine the next patient, when she felt a sense of dread come over her. She felt it had something to do with the baby girl she had delivered two weeks earlier. The baby was sickly, and Ida had spent many hours helping it survive until it was now strong and ready to go home later in the day. She wondered if God was trying to tell her something.

Ida jumped up from her chair. "I will be back in a moment," she said over her shoulder as she rushed for the door. Even as Ida did so, a voice in her head told her she was being ridiculous. The baby must be fine, or one of the workers would have come to fetch her. Still, she ran on until she came to the ward where the baby was. All seemed well as she stepped inside. Salomi was bent over a child feeding it, and the other babies all looked perfectly fine. Ida glanced over at the screened-off area where the little baby and her mother were. Since the feeling would not go away, she walked over and looked behind the screen.

"No! No!" she yelled as she saw the mother and grandmother standing over the baby, pressing a pillow firmly against its face. Startled, the pair looked up and loosened their grip. Ida reached for the baby, who was already turning blue. Desperately she massaged the child's chest, willing it to breathe. Finally she heard a small choking sound—the baby would live. Holding the child close to her, Ida turned to the mother and grandmother.

"How could you do this to an innocent child?" she asked. "You have plenty of money for her dowry when the time comes, and she is such a beautiful baby!"

The grandmother spat on the ground and raised her eyes defiantly to Ida. "She is better off dead. She was born on an unlucky day. It is the will of Allah that she die. We are merely carrying out his wishes.

If he did not wish her dead, why did he allow her to be born so unlucky?" the old woman snarled.

Ida was so furious she wanted to explode, but she controlled her temper. "I have worked hard to save her, and you want to destroy her. You can't really mean that she would be better off dead. Look at her—she is such a sweet little thing."

The grandmother's eyes squinted, and a sly smile came over her. "You don't want her to die?" she crooned. "Good. We wash our hands of her and the bad luck that will follow her. Take her. She is yours."

Ida's mind reeled. "But I...no, you can't mean..." she stuttered, trying to grasp the implications of what they were saying.

"You don't want the baby to be killed?" the grandmother repeated. "Then you take her. The cursed little thing is yours."

Ida looked at the young mother. Did she really want to give away her own baby?

"Yes, please take the baby from me. Perhaps next time Allah will allow me to give birth on a holy day," the mother said.

Indignation rose within Ida. "Every day a baby is born is a holy day!" she retorted, and then she looked down at the little girl snuggled in her arms. "Very well, if you want to give her away, I will take her."

With that Ida turned and walked out of the ward.

Chapter 9

Roadside

As Ida Scudder walked swiftly along the path that led to the bungalow she shared with her mother, the gravity of the situation hit her. She was now the "mother" of a two-week-old baby girl!

Ida found her own mother sorting pills on the back veranda.

"The grandmother was trying to kill this baby," Ida said simply, "and when I rescued it, they gave it to me."

"For good?" Sophia asked matter-of-factly.

"For good," Ida echoed. "What am I going to do with it?"

Ida's mother looked up and smiled. "The same thing any mother does with a little baby. Give it food and think of a name for it. Just take one step at a time, and things will work out fine."

Ida relaxed a little, thankful that her mother was at her side. Before the day was over, the baby had been named Mary Taber, after the hospital where she was born. Ida also found some local mothers who were willing to nurse Mary until she was old enough to take solid food.

That night, as Mary lay in a crib beside her bed, Ida said a special prayer of thanks to God for giving her the urge to check on the child just at the moment when the child was in peril. Ida hated to imagine what might have happened if she had not obeyed the urge to rush and check on the baby.

Under the care of Ida, her mother, and Annie, little Mary thrived. She became a smiling, chubby child, and she was soon joined by three other girls who were thrust upon Ida. While it was not Ida's idea to start a small orphanage, she could not turn away a baby in need. She tried to explain her growing clan in a letter to the mission board.

> I cannot refuse to take any child, no matter of how poor their birth or parentage, for we know that if they are surrounded by love and the right environment, they will grow up to be strong men and women: if we refuse to take them they will be sold to temples or houses of ill-fame to be brought up in the midst of the foulest sins. The Master took little

ones into His arms and loved and blessed them and we are trying to follow in His footsteps, and are gathering in all we can.

The children that Ida dreaded to see were those who had come to the hospital too late for her to help. One such child was a one-year-old boy. When his mother unwrapped the rags that covered him, Ida was repulsed to see a huge, running abscess on his left leg.

She turned to the mother and said, "What a pity! Why didn't you bring him to me sooner? He must have been in great pain for days."

The woman nodded. "That is true," she admitted, "but I could not bring him earlier. I did not dare. It was forbidden."

"Why?" Ida demanded.

"Because everyone told me that it was the image of a god growing on my son's leg and that I would anger the god if I touched it or let anyone remove it."

Ida did not trust herself to speak. Instead she picked up the little boy and carried him to the operating room, where she opened up the abscess. Just as she expected, it had grown inward as well as outward, and the boy's bone was infected. The boy would surely die, and Ida could do nothing to save him. With great sadness, she stitched him up and took him back to his mother.

That night Ida could not sleep. Thoughts of the dying little boy filled her mind. *Surely there must be something I can do about it,* she thought. *People in the villages need to know that there are other ways to treat disease.* The problem was not that there was no one in the village to act as a doctor. Quite the opposite was true: too many people claimed to have healing powers. Ida had been in India long enough to know that these "healers" fell into three categories.

The first group were the charm makers, who tied small pouches of crushed jackal's rib or swordfish spine around a sick person's neck and wrists and promised that they would ward off everything from smallpox to cholera.

The next category was more dangerous. These people were called "couchers," who specialized in operating on cataracts, a common cause of blindness in India, even among small children. For a fee and without sterilizing any equipment, the coucher would thrust a needle into the person's eye and push the hardened lens to one side. At first the patient could see better, but his or her better sight was quickly followed with inflammation and then complete, irreversible blindness. By then the coucher had moved on to the next village.

The third category was made up of those who sold strange potions and spells as a remedy for illness. The main problem here was that by the time patients realized that the potion or spell was doing no good, it was often too late for regular medical treatment to help them.

Yet Ida also knew that India had once led the world in medical knowledge. Sometime before 1000

B.C., an Indian physician named Dhanantari and his student Susruta had removed tumors, amputated limbs, fitted iron prostheses, and even experimented with skin grafting. They had an understanding of the need for sterile conditions and many other scientific ideas that would be lost for nearly three thousand years after they died. But while India had a wonderful medical heritage, Ida knew that what counted now was improving medical practice in the country.

Sometime before dawn Ida had an inspiration. If the village people were going to wait too long to come to her, she would go to them. She would hitch up a wagon at the hospital and take it out into the dustiest, dirtiest villages she could find. Louisa Hart was back in Vellore, along with her sister Lillian, a competent nurse, and they would be able to share this new workload between them. The plan came together with remarkable speed. A bandy was outfitted with shelves and a folding table, and within two weeks Ida was ready to go out on her first "Roadside," as she called this new venture.

Ida set out with faithful Salomi at her side. They traveled about five miles along a bumpy track and then stopped near a village. Two men sat by the road, and Ida called to them to come closer.

"We are from the hospital," she told them. "We want to help sick people. We will be back at the same time next week, and we will stop here. If you know anyone who is sick, tell them to wait for us here."

The older man's eye's lit up. "You will help me?" he said, thrusting out his right hand.

"If I can," Ida replied as she felt his pulse. She had learned long ago that every diagnosis in India begins with reading the pulse, on the right wrist of a man and the left wrist of a woman.

"I have flies buzzing in my ears," the man said. "I paid a doctor two annas to remove them, and he showed me a whole handful of flies that he took out of my ear. But he told me he would need another two annas to remove the rest of them. I do not have the money. But could you take the rest of the flies out for me?"

Ida pulled out her medical bag, found a magnifying glass, and peered into the man's ear, where she saw a pebble embedded against his eardrum. No wonder he was hearing buzzing in his ear. Ida carefully removed the pebble with a pair of tweezers and sent the man on his way marveling at how she had silenced the flies in his ear without removing them.

Ida and Salomi continued on their way, treating patients they found and spreading the word that they would return to the same place in a week's time. The following week small crowds were waiting at each Roadside stop. The high-caste Hindus waited on one side of the road, and the poor and Muslims waited on the other side. Not wanting to miss the opportunity to share the gospel message, Ida opened every Roadside with prayer and invited people to ask her questions about the Christian faith. By the end of the year, the team of doctors and nurses at the Mary Taber Schell Memorial Hospital were treating approximately thirty thousand outpatients both in the clinic and at the Roadsides.

Once again Ida began to dream. This time it was not a hospital she envisioned but a nursing school to train young Indian women. It would take buildings, teachers, and money to make the nursing school a reality. Suddenly Ida felt the urge to return to the United States, where she could explain her plans for the nursing school and raise money to get it started. And the sooner she got it started the better!

In the summer of 1907 Ida, her mother, and Annie set sail for America. Ida left Mary and the other orphan children in Salomi's capable care.

Once the women arrived in the United States, Annie went her separate way for a year of fundraising and visiting family, friends, and supporters. Ida and her mother headed to Nebraska for a family reunion on the farm where Ida had spent some of her childhood. It was wonderful to see so many family members again. Her brother Lewis and his wife, Cora, still lived on the farm. As the rest of the family gathered, they borrowed tents to accommodate everyone. All of Ida's brothers—John, Lewis, Charles, Henry, and Walter—were there, along with their wives and an assortment of children.

Ida met many of her nieces and nephews for the first time, including her namesake, Ida Belle Scudder, the seven-year-old daughter of Lewis and Cora. Little, blond Ida Belle looked a lot like the elder Ida when she was young, but she was much more shy. As the family took cart rides and picnicked by the creek, Ida often found Ida Belle sitting beside her waiting for another story about her aunt's life and work in India. Ida was amazed at how long the little girl would sit and listen as she described operations and diseases in detail. Perhaps, she told herself, Ida Belle might one day take on her profession as well as her name.

The lazy, sunny days on the farm soon ended, and it was time for Ida to return to New York, where she had enrolled in some postgraduate classes. While she was there, she stayed with Gertrude Dodd, the woman who had financed Annie Hancock's way to India seven years before. Since that time Ida and Gertrude had written to each other many times, and Ida was eager to see Gertrude in person again.

The three-month course in New York sped by. When it was over, Ida went on a speaking tour of the east coast of the United States and Canada, telling stories and raising money for the new nursing school she hoped to open when she returned.

By the time she got back to New York, Ida had pledges for five thousand dollars toward the school. Better yet, she had met Delia Houghton, a registered nurse who was eager and competent to take on the task of being the nursing school's first instructor. Ida was delighted that not only was Delia going back to India with her, but Katharine Van Nest, whom Ida had lived with for a time in New York eight years before, and Gertrude had decided to accompany her to India to see conditions there for themselves.

On November 12, 1908, Ida stood at the stern of the SS *Cedric* as it steamed out of New York Harbor. Beside her on deck were her mother, Annie Hancock, Gertrude Dodd, Katharine Van Nest, and Delia Houghton. As Ida looked at the five women watching New York City slip from view, she smiled to herself. She wondered what six strong women with faith in God and a determination to make a difference in the lives of females in India could accomplish in the months and years ahead.

Chapter 10

An Animal-less Carriage

The voyage to India gave the six women plenty of time to plan, and by the time they reached Madras, preparations were well under way for the Vellore Nursing School. Ida had anticipated some problems getting the school up and running, and she was right. The women had decided to accept only high-school graduates into the program, but few females in India met this requirement. And of the few who met the requirement, most were married as soon as they finished high school or went into the teaching profession. Ida sent word to all of the missions in the area, asking them to find suitable young women to apply for the nursing school.

Slowly applications began to trickle in. About half of them came from Christians, and the rest were from Hindus and Muslims. This suited Ida fine. She wanted the college to be open to women of all faiths. By the end of 1908, the nursing school was fully operating, with fifteen students enrolled.

Eventually Gertrude and Katharine returned to the United States as planned, but they left with a new determination to spread the word about the good work going on at Vellore. Meanwhile Delia, after completing a Tamil language course, turned out to be a capable nursing school director.

Soon Ida was able to turn her attention back to the Roadsides. While Ida had been away in the United States, two of the Roadside stops had evolved into regular clinics, one at Gudiyattam, twenty-three miles away, and one even farther away, at Punganur.

Ida loved this work, but the bumpy bandy ride was a grueling experience, and Ida often prayed for a more efficient way to reach the people. Her answer came in the form of a letter from someone who had heard her speak in the United States. When she opened the letter, Ida read the most amazing news. The writer was sending her an automobile, a Peugeot, so that she could visit the more remote villages with ease.

A Peugeot! It took a while for the idea of getting a motorcar to sink in. While she had been in the United States, Ida had been driven in several of them, but they were new and unknown things to her. She had never seen one in or around Vellore, and she wondered how the local people would take to an "animal-less carriage."

On September 23, 1909, a huge wooden crate was unloaded at Ida's door. Inside it was the motorcar—or rather all the parts to construct the motorcar, if someone could be found who knew how to go about putting it together.

Ida wrote to missionaries in Madras, and they found a mechanic who assured everyone that he was capable of putting the Peugeot together. Ida, along with half the town, watched eagerly as the mechanic assembled the car. When it was finished, it had a folding top, hard leather seats, a loud horn, and a one-cylinder engine.

A week later, on September 30, the Peugeot was tested and ready for its first Roadside visit. Ida sat beside Hussain, the driver, while Salomi and a female Bible teacher sat in the backseat, almost hidden beneath all the bags of drugs and bandages. Hussain could not seem to stop swerving, and the canvas bags filled with additional supplies thumped wildly against the sides of the windshield.

A group of field workers farther down the road spotted the car coming and ran off into the field screaming, "The devil is coming! The devil is coming!"

Ida ordered Hussain to stop the car. She ran into the field after the workers, hoping to explain that it was just an oxenless bandy and would not harm them. But the workers were too shocked to listen to her.

Others had the same reaction. At Roadside after Roadside, people fled from the car. Ida found that the only way she could keep her patients in one place long enough to treat them was to stop the car some distance before each Roadside and walk the rest of the way.

Still, Ida was not too discouraged. She hoped that the people would soon come to accept the strange sight of an automobile and that Hussain's steering precision would quickly improve.

Ida continued her Roadsides, and within a few weeks, the crowds were back. Once they accepted that the car was not going to hurt them, the people were eager to investigate every inch of it. It was not long before the horn was missing, but that did not matter much. Since this was the only motorized vehicle for miles around, no one had any trouble recognizing Ida's car by the sound of its spluttering engine.

Ida was glad to see that people in the villages understood that the car enabled her to cover more ground in a day and treat more patients. She knew that people appreciated the car every time the Peugeot met its match at the Katpadi Railway Over-bridge. This bridge was high, and the car did not have the horsepower to make it more than halfway up the steep incline to the overpass. Each time it wheezed to a stop, nearby bullock drivers and merchants would rush out to push the Peugeot over the hump and watch it coast down the incline on the other side of the bridge.

By Christmas Ida was treating over three hundred people a day at her Roadsides. Many of the patients had never before seen a medical doctor, and they had little idea of how to follow instructions. When Ida gave one man some cotton wadding, he asked if he was supposed to eat it to make his ear better. One woman laughed when Ida washed her hands before performing a roadside operation. "What's the point of that? Everyone knows your hands will get dirty again," she said. Ida was patient with the people's ignorance and took every opportunity to explain to them why they should follow her advice.

One opportunity came soon after Christmas when the Peugeot broke down near Elavampadi, a village where Ida had not stopped before. Realizing that she would have to get the mechanic from Madras to fix the problem, Ida walked into Elavampadi to hire a bandy to take her to visit patients. The normally shy inhabitants beckoned Ida into their homes to show her the illness that afflicted many of them. Ida knew what it was right away: the guinea worm, a two to three-foot-long parasite that gets into the bloodstream and eats its way through the flesh to the outside to lay its eggs. The area around the guinea worm's exit point becomes swollen and abscessed, and Ida could see the thin white worm writhing just beneath the skin of some people.

Appalled as she was, Ida tried to keep smiling and promised to come back the following week to show the people how to rid their town of the worm. Many of the people of the village found it hard to believe that there was a cure for this thing that had been a scourge for generations. But when Ida returned the next week, they welcomed her.

Ida did not come back alone. She had made the guinea worm the subject of a nursing school lecture, and each of the students had drawn up a chart to show how the worm continues its cycle of infecting humans. On this visit Ida brought along with her the top student to explain the guinea worm to the people of Elavampadi, who had all gathered in the schoolhouse to listen.

It was simple, really. The worm larvae bred in water, and when people drank this infected water, the tiny worms entered the body and continued to grow. When the student nurse had given her presentation, Ida stood up and beckoned to two small boys in the front row. She handed them each an empty beaker and said, "Here, go to the village's two wells and collect a cup full of water from each and bring it back to me."

The two boys raced off and returned several minutes later with water from both wells. Ida looked in the beakers and nodded.

"I will pass these around," she said. "If you look very carefully, you will see tiny white bugs moving in the water. These are really the baby worms, and drinking this water is how they get into your bodies."

She waited for several minutes while all those gathered dutifully examined the beakers and exclaimed that they could, in fact, see something wiggling around in them.

When everyone had examined the beakers, Ida went on. "There are two ways to get rid of the worms in the water," she began. "One way is to boil the water, but it would take a lot of firewood, and I know that you do not have much of that here. The other way is to take a clean piece of cloth"—she paused to pull a handkerchief from her pocket— "and pour the well water through it. The cloth will catch all the worms. Then lay the cloth in the sun to kill the worms."

Several people started talking at once, and the meeting broke into small groups. But Ida hoped that she and the nursing school student had made their point. Straining the water was such a simple thing to do, yet it would prevent so much infection and even some deaths.

The following week Ida was delighted to learn that there were no new outbreaks of guinea worm in Elavampadi and that villagers were reminding each other to strain the water.

It was a good outcome, but since there were many other times when Ida felt powerless to break through ancient Indian traditions, she tried to find other ways around them. Hindus in particular felt it was wrong to give anyone with a fever a drink of water, which meant that some patients actually died of thirst in their own homes. Ida got tired of pleading with the people to change their ways and started prescribing large quantities of "medicine" for patients with fever. She made the medicine by mixing a tiny amount of quinine in a pitcher of water. The quinine gave the water a bitter, medicinal taste. Then, for added effect, Ida added a few drops of potassium permanganate to turn the liquid a purple color. Soon some of the worst cases of dehydration were being cured by cup after cup of this magic "medicine."

At times villages were closed to Ida because the Hindus living in them were of high caste and did not want to be polluted by her touch. Again Ida tried to be patient and prayed for the right opportunity to break down the prejudice against her.

One village that was closed to her was Lathery. Even though Ida often stopped on the outskirts of the village, no one came to greet her until one February day when, much to Ida's surprise, eight men approached the car. *Between them they were leading a sick bullock!*

Knowing that a bullock could bring in the only income for a family, Ida agreed to examine it. This proved difficult, because every time she approached the huge animal, it stamped its feet and flared its nostrils. After several unsuccessful attempts, the men came to the rescue. They flipped the bullock over on its side and sat on it while Ida did her examination. She spotted a tumor in the outer ear and quickly removed it over the protests of the bullock. As soon as Ida was done, the bullock roused itself to its feet and tugged to get away from her.

All that week Ida wondered whether the bullock was still alive and making a good recovery. At the next Roadside, Hussain stopped the car at the outskirts of Lathery. Many people came out to welcome Ida, yelling that the bullock was in fine health and that they had several people who needed help too. Ida was delighted that a sick bullock had made a way for another village to be open to medical treatment and the gospel, which she always shared with her patients.

The work continued to expand, and by the end of 1910, Ida was exhausted. The mission board stretched the few doctors it had as far as possible, and Louisa Hart was reassigned to Madanapalle, leaving forty-year-old Ida to carry on alone at the hospital and Roadsides. By the time summer arrived, Ida had to admit that something drastic needed to be done about the situation. There was no way for her mission board, or any other mission board, for that matter, to supply enough doctors to meet the needs of the Indian people.

As Ida traveled to Kodaikanal to attend a medical conference, a question formed in her mind. What if she started a medical college to train women doctors at Vellore? All the way up the mountain, Ida mulled over the idea. Part of her knew that it was outrageous to think of a medical college when everyone was stretched to the limit trying to run the hospital and nursing school. But another part of her believed that if it could be done, it could help solve the current shortage of doctors and train Indians for generations to come.

Ida finally made up her mind when she visited her father's grave. She asked herself what he would have advised her to do, and she felt sure that he would have told her to reach for the stars, that Jesus promised that people could move mountains if they only believed.

Once Ida had made up her mind to pursue a medical school for women, her next challenge was to work out how to make it happen. She decided to speak her mind at the Kodaikanal Missionary Medical Conference, an interdenominational meeting of foreign doctors who served in southern India. When the day of the meeting arrived, Ida could hardly contain herself. She was certain that everyone should work together to see a medical training center started.

When the chairman of the meeting asked for comments, Ida jumped to her feet and announced her idea. She watched as eyebrows were raised and other doctors began whispering to each other. When she had given all the reasons she could think of for a new college, she sat down beside her cousin Lew Scudder, who leaned over and spoke softly to her.

"I wish you had talked to me first, Ida," Lew began. "Really, I don't see how your idea is practical. All of the mission boards are short on money, and none of them will want to put what they have into an interdenominational project, I am sure of that."

A doctor to Ida's right joined in. "Women doctors? Even if you did get the money, it's impossible. Indian women won't become doctors. Their families won't let them. Ida, be reasonable. There are already seven medical colleges for men in South India. Train your nurses and leave it at that," he said.

Ida tried not to take such remarks personally. She had expected opposition, but deep down it still stung. Only two doctors, the only other women in the room, encouraged her idea, and together the three of them were able to push for a committee to study Ida's suggestion.

The committee was scheduled to research the proposal and report back to the conference during the summer of the following year, 1912. Ida was impatient to get something started sooner, but she contented herself with walking around the area that she felt would be a good site for the new college. The site was about four miles south of Vellore, on the Arni road. For some reason no one lived or farmed in the lush valley nestled between rocky hills. Ida loved the spot, especially the backdrop—a majestic mountain named Kailasa.

As Ida walked over the land and prayed for the college, she could imagine tall buildings with wide verandas and students weary from study gazing out picture windows at the magnificent scenery.

It was a restless year for Ida, who kept busy opening a tuberculosis sanitarium at Punganur, took on the responsibility of several more babies and abandoned children, and expanded the hospital from forty-three beds to sixty. But always, in the back of her mind, was the question of how the committee was doing and what its findings would be.

Finally the year passed, and during the summer of 1912, Ida received the answer she had prayed for but hardly dared believe. With the constant encouragement of the other two female doctors, the committee had agreed that a union medical college for women in South India was a good idea.

Ida did not allow herself to get too excited, however. It was a small beginning. The committee still had to approve a location for the college, obtain permission from the government, and then convince four struggling denominational mission boards to work together. And then there was the matter of raising the money needed to build the new college and recruit staff and students for it.

Most people, even Ida's mother, tried to convince Ida to drop the whole idea. Mrs. Scudder told Ida that she was already carrying the workload of three doctors. But Ida was consumed with thoughts of a medical college for women. When she shut her eyes, she could see lines of women in white saris receiving their diplomas and then going out in their hundreds to work among the women of India. Yes, she could see it all, but how was she going to make it happen?

Chapter 11

"So You Are the Woman?"

Although Ida dreamed of a medical school, she was realistic enough to know that it could take years to happen. In the meantime there was an urgent need for more hospital space. Ida set her sights on that problem. She visited government officials in Madras and asked them for a grant to add 150 more beds. The officials turned down her request, explaining that they gave grants only to educational institutions, not to hospitals. Ida thought this was ridiculous. To her the hospital, the Roadsides, the outlying clinics—all played a vital role in educating rural Indians about their health. And what of the nurses who trained in the hospital? Eighteen had graduated and now worked full-time at the hospital.

Ida returned several times to Madras to press her point, and eventually the government relented. The officials promised that the government would fund one third of the amount needed to enlarge the hospital, up to a maximum of twenty thousand dollars. Ida was ecstatic. Now all she had to do was raise the matching forty thousand dollars on her next furlough.

More good news followed. The mission board of the Reformed Church voted to buy the land necessary to expand the existing hospital. And in May 1914, at a conference of the South India Medical Association, four denominations voted to work together to one day build and run a medical school for women. The school was to be located in Vellore, with Ida as its principal. The funds to start the new venture would be raised in the United States and Great Britain.

In July 1914 Ida and her mother boarded a ship headed for the United States and furlough. Throughout the voyage Ida's mind was alive with ways to present the needs of Indian women to Americans. Ida could never have imagined, as the ship steamed its way toward the East Coast of the United States, that something was about to dash her hopes of raising all the money she needed to complete the hospital expansion.

When Ida and her mother disembarked in New York, shocking news awaited. Europe was at war! Although President Woodrow Wilson declared that the United States would remain neutral, many

Americans were focused on the bloody battlefields of Europe and gave money to the Red Cross and other war-related charities rather than to a hospital expansion project in India.

Ida did the best she could, often speaking four times a day. She drew heavily on the moral support of Katharine Van Nest, Gertrude Dodd, and Lucy Peabody, another woman who had visited Vellore to see conditions there for herself. Ida wondered how she could have gone on without these three women to buoy up her spirits.

By fall 1915 Ida knew she had to return to India, whether she had the money for the expansion or not. In fact, she had been able to raise only eight thousand dollars, which, along with the Indian government's grant, meant that she had a total of twelve thousand dollars to put toward the expansion project. Ida comforted herself with the fact that at least it was enough to make a start on the project.

By now the high seas had become a dangerous battleground, with Germany warning Americans against sailing across the Atlantic Ocean. To underscore their point, the Germans sank a British liner, the *Lusitania*, causing the death of over twelve hundred people, including one hundred twenty-eight Americans. As she prepared to set sail herself, Ida wondered how long the American government could stall before it, too, declared war on Germany. Thankfully, the voyage back to India was uneventful, and Ida and her mother arrived safely back in Madras.

Once back in Vellore, Ida plunged again into work, lecturing to nurses, operating on patients, and conducting Roadsides. Every so often news of the progress of the Great War in Europe reached as far as Vellore. One source of news was Gertrude, who had been so impressed with the needs of India that she arrived in Vellore soon after Ida returned, not for a visit but to stay for good. Gertrude cheerfully announced that she had sold her New York apartment, had said farewell to her family and friends, and was prepared to spend the rest of her life helping to fulfill Ida's vision for Indian women.

Ida was stunned, and delighted. Gertrude was a special friend and a wonderful administrator. Within weeks she had taken over managing the hospital accounts, something that had been a constant headache to Ida.

In January 1916, four months after Ida's return from the United States, the building committee appointed by the South India Medical Association arrived in Vellore to inspect the two hundred-acre site on Arni Road. Much to Ida's delight, the committee approved the site. Ida had been eyeing the site for a long time, and now she could almost see the medical school there. However, a few obstacles stood in the way. The main one was the price tag for the school. When everything was added up, to build a facility that would meet government standards would cost one million dollars!

The difficulties involved in raising the small sum of eight thousand dollars while on furlough were still fresh in Ida's mind. Yet Ida refused to let the huge amount needed for the medical college daunt her. Somehow, she told herself, God would provide the money. In the meantime Ida had plenty to do supervising the hospital extension and building a dispensary in the village. More doctors arrived from the United States to help out, despite the fact that the United States had entered the Great War in early 1917 and the U. S. Army was putting a lot of pressure on doctors to enlist.

By 1918 the hospital extension was complete, and Ida once again had time to focus on her dream of building a medical school. She made a trip to Madras to talk with Colonel Bryson, the head of the British Medical Department for the Madras region. The colonel had already heard of the proposal for the medical school, and he revealed an amused smile as he invited Ida into his office. A ceiling fan beat the humid air overhead as the colonel guided Ida to a straight-backed wooden chair opposite his desk.

"So," he began as he took his seat behind the expansive mahogany desk, "you are the woman who actually thinks she is going to start a medical school in Vellore?"

"Yes," Ida replied, aware that she was holding her head a little higher than normal. She looked Colonel Bryson in the eye. "It will be a wonderful addition to the area's medical facilities, don't you think?"

"If it ever happens, surely," the colonel replied. "But I don't believe you have any buildings, do you?"

"Not yet," Ida replied, "but we have decided to rent some houses near the hospital in which to hold the school until the structure on Arni Road is finally built."

"And money?" Colonel Bryson continued, playing with his fountain pen.

"We are working on it. As you know, this is not a good time to raise money in the United States or England, but the money will come."

"And staff?"

Ida felt like reaching out and grabbing the colonel by his collar. He was toying with her, but she remained patient with him.

"I am qualified to teach most of the subjects at a first-year level," she said. "The girls can attend physics and chemistry classes at Voorhees College in Vellore, our mission's college for young men. Once things get moving, word will travel, and other doctors will come to join the teaching staff." Ida's voice was confident and firm.

"Let me get this right. You have no buildings, no money, and no staff," Colonel Bryson mused, "and you think you are ready to start a medical school. It would be ridiculous if it weren't so…" —he looked at Ida and searched for the right word— "so heroic."

"It's not about being heroic," Ida countered. "It's about a huge need out there that we have to find a way to fill. You, Colonel, above all should understand that."

Ida studied Colonel Bryson's face to see if she had offended him, but apparently she had not.

"You are right about that," the colonel conceded. "But even if you had the building, the money, and the staff, we are talking about *Indian* women training to be doctors." He shook his head. "You know how hard it is to find qualified applicants to be nurses. I just don't see it happening. Especially when, once they are trained, they will have to compete against top Indian men from seven medical schools."

"You don't think women have the brains to be doctors?" Ida retorted.

"Obviously you made it, and I have the utmost respect for you. But I doubt that *Indian* women could achieve what you have."

Ida kept her anger in check. Colonel Bryson had the power to kill or promote the idea of a medical school for women, and she was determined to find a way to reach him. Perhaps, she thought, she should try humor.

"Well," she said, forcing a big smile on her face, "have you heard the story about the dinner served in India, at which one of the courses was to be sheep's brains?"

"No, I haven't," the colonel replied.

"When the meal was served, that course was omitted. Later the mistress asked the cook what had happened to the dish of sheep's brains. 'O, madam,' the cook replied, 'the sheep they butchered for me was a female, and it had no brains.'"

Colonel Bryson laughed, and the tension subsided. "All right, Dr. Scudder, you'll be fortunate if you get three applications," he said, "but if you get six, go ahead and start your school. You have the permission of the government."

Ida managed to stay composed while she chatted with Colonel Bryson for a few minutes more, but once she was out of his earshot, she let out a whoop of delight! Her medical school had been approved! She was on her way.

No time was lost in sending out a prospectus for the new school to all missionary and government high schools and colleges for girls in the Madras region. The prospectus announced that students must be over eighteen, have good grades in their final exams, speak and write English, and have character references. It also informed would-be applicants that the school was open to all women regardless of religion or caste.

Once the flyers had been put in the mail, Ida was not finished. She visited many schools herself, seeking out intelligent young women whose families were willing to let them train to be doctors.

At a Methodist school in Tinnevelly, Ida gave her usual promotional speech and answered questions. As she got up to leave, she noticed one girl lingering behind. The principal of the school noticed her too.

"She is one of our brightest students," she whispered to Ida. "If you can interest her, she will be a credit to you."

Ida saw something about the girl, perhaps her alert look, that attracted her, and she walked over to talk to the student.

"I've had my eye on you during the presentation, and I think you would make a great doctor," Ida said forthrightly.

The girl looked shocked. "You do?" she replied.

Ida reached out and held the girl's hands up for inspection. "Yes. You have strong hands and long fingers. And you obviously like to observe things, just as much as I do. What is your name?"

"Ebbie," the girl quietly replied. "Ebbie Gnanamuthu."

"What a nice name," Ida said. "Would you like to be a doctor, Ebbie?"

"I...I don't know," Ebbie stammered. "I'm not sure I would be good enough."

Ida smiled. "Humility is a good trait for a doctor."

As Ida and the principal walked to Ida's new Model T motorcar, Ida learned that Ebbie, short for Ebenezer, came from a very poor Christian family. Ebbie's father, who earned about seven dollars a month, was a pastor. The principal was convinced that Ebbie would make a good doctor, as was Ida. Soon it was arranged that a scholarship be given to Ebbie if she found the courage to apply for the medical college.

Ebbie did apply, along with sixty-nine other young women! Ida could hardly wait to see Colonel Bryson again and let him know. Six students indeed!

Then came the painful job of selecting seventeen students, the best and most dedicated from the group of applicants. Much to Ida's delight, one student who made the final cut was Ebbie Gnanamuthu.

Now that Ida had her students, she needed a facility in which to teach and house them all. She rented several bungalows in the village and scrubbed out a shed to use as a dissection room. Then she turned her attention to equipment, of which there was little—two books, one microscope, and one skeleton.

Ingenuity was needed, and Ida had plenty of that. She bought lengths of colored ribbon and attached them to the wired-together skeleton. She used red to show where the arteries were, blue for veins, and yellow for nerves. Then she used cloth and padding to make muscles, and even rigged them up so that they would flex when she pulled a string.

The medical college was officially opened on August 12, 1918. The governor of Madras and Colonel Bryson were both in attendance. In his speech the colonel told the young women, "I wonder if you realize what important people you are. Fifty years hence you will remind the students of that generation that you were among those present at the opening of this school. It is an honor that none can ever share with you."

A week later Ida was sure that some of the students wondered whether it was an honor after all. Ida taught chapel at 7:30 each morning, reading selections from the New Testament. She especially liked to read 1 Corinthians 13, which she read aloud every Monday morning to remind the women how to start off their week well. Classes were held from eight to ten in the morning. Then the students all followed Ida to the hospital, where they watched as she made her rounds of the wards. In the previous few years, anatomy had undergone a "modernization." In her day Ida had learned about thirty thousand anatomical terms while in medical school. Now many of those terms had been replaced with newer ones, which meant that the students now had to learn both the old and the new terms, some fifty thousand of them in all. Ida gave a test every Friday, and she graded harshly. Anyone who scored below 90 percent failed.

It was not the tests that were the most daunting to the young women, but dealing with bodies and blood. Most of the students had a horror of touching blood, and many times Ida had to stop her lesson for a few minutes while someone revived a student who had fainted. The local jail provided Ida with two dead bodies for the class to dissect, which proved to be a tremendous challenge for everyone. Ebbie, one of Ida's favorite students, was deathly afraid of the sight of blood and begged to be allowed to go home. She even wrote to her sister asking her to come and take her away. But Ida would not hear of it. "No," she said, "you have too much potential; you must stay and toughen up."

Ida realized that these young women were attempting something that had never before been done in Indian culture, and she helped them as best she could. But she also understood that, in the end, to get respect, they had to be as good as or better than their male counterparts. And so the women worked hard. Ida gave her students the opportunity to play hard too. She set up badminton and tennis courts for them to play on in the evenings, and sometimes all seventeen of them piled into the Model T Ford with Ida for a jaunt into the countryside.

The students worked in the hospital and at the Roadsides seven days a week. They had time off for church on Sunday but were expected to do their various duties after that. "Sunday is God's day," Ida would tell them, "and this is God's work, so we need to do it especially well on Sunday."

Ida worked harder than they all did, and many Indian people marveled at the dedication she showed to her adopted land. In September she received official notification that she was to be awarded the Kaisar-i-Hind award given by King George V for public service to India. This was quite an honor, especially as Ida was to be given the gold medal first-class. The ceremony in Government House in Madras was a glittering affair, attended by eight hundred of the most prominent people in South India. The silk dresses and diamond tiaras would have once awed Ida, but now she was more interested in seeking out people who could help promote rural health care and her medical school for women.

By Christmas three of the students had dropped out, one through illness, one to get married, and one because she found the work too difficult. The

fourteen who remained told Ida they were determined to stay and graduate.

Three months after the school started, there was
more than enough work for everyone. The war in
Europe had come to an end in November, but
another killer followed on its heels. A great influenza
epidemic swept around the world. Vellore was not
spared. The local people had never seen a disease
like it, and many of them turned to their gods. In
village after village, they hung out old rags and broken baskets, hoping that the goddess of death would
see these items and deem their village unworthy of
her presence.

At the hospital both patients and staff were hit
hard. The head nurse of the hospital died, as did six
of the other nurses. They were people Ida could not
afford to lose, but somehow the survivors carried on.

Eventually the epidemic subsided, and May 1919
rolled around. It was time for Ida to accompany her
students to Madras for their first-year medical examinations. As they all bundled on the train together,
Ida was sure she was more nervous than her students were. She tried to distract herself by looking
out the window, but doubts kept filling her mind.
What if Colonel Bryson was right? She knew the
girls had tried their hardest, but was it enough to
compete against the brightest young men in India,
all of whom were trained at well-equipped medical
colleges? Ida did not know. And meeting Colonel
Bryson in the hallway soon after she arrived didn't
help ease her mind.

"My dear doctor," the colonel told Ida, "please don't be discouraged if none of your students makes the grade the first time."

"None of them?" Ida repeated in horror.

The colonel's voice softened. "It wouldn't be surprising. It's a very difficult exam. Only about 20 percent of the men pass, and naturally we can't expect too much of your young women." He smiled. "But they can always try again."

Try again! Ida thought. These fourteen women had worked as hard as humanly possible. If some of them did not pass, Ida had no idea what they could do differently next time around.

Chapter 12

The Top Medical School in the District

When the examinations were over, Ida and her students returned to Vellore to await the results. Ida prayed that some of the girls would pass. It would be discouraging if not a single student made it to the second year.

Three weeks later Ida received a letter from Colonel Bryson. Her hands shook as she opened it. She gasped as she read down the list of names. Ebbie, pass. Thai, pass. Saramma, pass. Anna, pass. Her eyes scanned to the bottom of the sheet. Every one of the girls had passed! The men's colleges had a 20 percent pass rate, but the Vellore medical college had a 100 percent pass rate. Ida ran to find the girls so they could all celebrate together.

"You did it. You all did it," she told them excitedly. "And can you believe it? We came in top of all the medical schools in the district!"

Ida found it hard to believe this herself. The next time she saw Colonel Bryson, he sheepishly shook her hand.

"I'm afraid, Dr. Scudder," he said awkwardly, "that your girls are setting too high a standard for our men to live up to."

Ida smiled and said nothing.

Word traveled fast, and that year there were twice as many students applying to the best medical college in the Madras region. Ida accepted twenty-five of them, bringing the total number of students enrolled to thirty-nine. Since government regulations required three hospital beds for each student, Ida had to increase the number of hospital beds to 117. This was no easy feat, and the verandas had to be pressed into service as wards. The need to expand the hospital still further was more urgent than ever.

The number of orphans Ida had taken in and now cared for had grown too. They now numbered twenty-three, ranging in age from six months to sixteen years.

As the needs of the mission grew, Ida eagerly received letters from Lucy Peabody in the United States. Lucy was raising money for Vellore and other missions that helped women throughout Asia. As the money that Lucy had raised came in, Ida was able to begin a building program at Thotapalayam, two miles away from Schell Hospital. There Ida watched impatiently as a chapel, a children's ward, and a maternity hospital began to take shape.

Money trickled in for the project until February 1921, when Ida received some wonderful news. Lucy wrote to tell her that the Laura Spelman Rockefeller Memorial Fund had offered one million dollars to be shared among the seven planned and existing Asian universities for women that Lucy raised money for. There was just one catch. Lucy and her committee had to come up with matching funds of two million dollars before the end of 1922! It wasn't difficult to do the math. Two million plus one million was three million dollars divided among seven institutions, which meant that each institution would receive $425,000. Ida knew just what she could do with that amount of money, and she arranged to go back to the United States to help raise it.

Before that, however, the first class of medical students graduated in March 1922. It was a day Ida would never forget. The nursing students braided thick chains of jasmine and ferns and formed an aisle for the fourteen students to walk along. Colonel Bryson was there to hand out the diplomas and offer congratulations to the women and to compliment Ida.

"She is a woman not only of vision but also of persistence," he told the group. "'Medical school, medical school, medical school...' She kept saying it. And she has not been oversilent, overmodest in her demands!"

Everyone laughed, including Ida. She knew she'd had to push Colonel Bryson to allow her to start the medical school, but as she looked from woman to woman, she knew it had all been worthwhile.

In front of her stood Ebbie Gnanamuthu, the girl who had been terrified of the sight of blood and begged to be allowed to leave the school. Now Ebbie had won the Government of India's gold medal in anatomy, and most of her fellow students had also won top awards. And better yet for Ida, fifty-two more students were watching the ceremony, dreaming of their own graduation.

Ida was due to leave for furlough in the United States in less than two months, and the graduation ceremony was a wonderful note to leave Vellore on.

Ida, her mother, who was now eighty years old, and Gertrude set sail together on May 5, 1922. This time they left from Bombay, and as the ship chugged its way to Boston, it made only one stop along the way, in Aden. Ida did not care. The sooner she met with Lucy and helped with the fundraising efforts, the happier she would be. By the time the ship steamed into Boston Harbor, Ida had just six months left to raise the money before the end-of-year deadline.

This time Ida did not feel that she could spend time on the farm in Nebraska with her extended family. Instead, two of her brothers met the women when the ship docked and took Mrs. Scudder away for a vacation. Ida and Gertrude went straight to work. They met with Lucy, who was doing all she could to raise the money. Lucy had marshaled a group of women from ten denominations in the United States and Canada, and the women called themselves the Committee for the Women's Union Christian Colleges of the Orient. From what Ida could gather, the women had worked tirelessly, but they were still well short of the two million dollars needed.

Ida added her weight to the campaign, traveling from New York to Michigan to Ohio and Minnesota. Everywhere she went, her message was the same. There were more than 165 million women and girls in India and only 159 female doctors to care for them. The Western world could never send over enough qualified women doctors to serve all of these people, and Indian women were ready and able to take up the challenge; they just needed support from the West to get going. The message hit home, but in her quiet moments, even Ida had to admit that two million dollars was an unprecedented amount to raise.

Thankfully, Ida did not have many quiet moments. She was too busy organizing events such as College Days, where she urged colleges in the United States to adopt sister colleges from the seven they were raising money for.

The weeks passed swiftly as Ida and the others raced against the clock to come up with the money. On December 9, 1922, Ida's fifty-second birthday, they held Dollar Day, where they urged thousands of people to give a dollar each to the cause. This was a successful event but not successful enough, and on December 31, 1922, Lucy came to Ida in tears.

"It's no use. Our time has run out, and we have done all we can, but we are fifty thousand dollars short," she sobbed.

Even when news came that the Rockefeller Foundation had extended the deadline by a month, Lucy held out little hope that the money would be raised. Still, she went on a scheduled fundraising trip to California, where she met an elderly women who wrote a check for the last fifty thousand dollars—on January 31, 1923, the last day of the extension.

When Ida and Gertrude Dodd heard the news, they could barely contain their excitement. The next day the *New York Times* blazed the headline: "$3,000,000 ASSURED TO SCHOOLS IN EAST. Church Women Win $2,000,000 Campaign and Rockefellers Give the Rest." It was the headline so many women had prayed and worked toward. Now that the money was assured, Ida was eager to get back to India and turn the new funds into buildings.

In her usual style, Ida had kept her eye out for potential staff as she traveled around, and she was delighted to meet a young doctor named Carol Jameson, who had graduated from Stanford University. Carol was currently doing a year's internship at the Mayo Clinic in Minnesota, but her eyes lit up when Ida told her about Vellore, and she promised to join the staff there as soon as her internship was up.

Carol arrived at Vellore in October 1923, and Ida set her straight to work. Like so many other Westerners, Dr. Carol, as she was called, was shocked by what passed as "medicine." She cringed when she unwrapped a serious wound and found that it had been "treated" with ashes from a fire and neem leaves, then bound in a filthy rag. Ida patiently explained to her how their role as doctors was to overcome ignorance with knowledge while keeping an eye out for any Indian practices that had medicinal value.

In November Ida took Dr. Carol with her to show her how to conduct a Roadside. She knew it would be overwhelming at first, especially for a young graduate who had worked at the Mayo Clinic, one of the top medical facilities in the United States. It was hard to imagine a greater contrast than between the sterile, businesslike conditions of the clinic and the dusty, chaotic setting of the Roadside. Dr. Carol watched Ida at the first two stops and then jumped right in to help out. As usual, the number of patients seemed to expand to fit the number of medical workers, and it was late in the afternoon before Ida headed the Model T for home.

By now Ida loved to drive the car herself. She was just pulling away from the side of the road when she spotted a woman leading three men across the rice fields toward them. For a brief moment Ida was tempted to slam her foot on the accelerator and leave before they reached her, but she could not. Instead she stopped the car, got out, and waited until they came closer.

As the men stumbled along the mud banks that separated the rice paddies, Ida realized that they must all be blind.

"We are coming," the woman yelled as she waved to Ida. "Please wait."

Ida waved back, and Dr. Carol got out of the car. Soon the three blind men were standing in front of them. They were exhausted but jubilant.

"We walked all night to get here in time. We were afraid we would miss you, but we have not," one of the men laughed. "We have made it. We hear that you can cure blindness."

"We will first have to see what the problem is," Ida said as she reached out and examined the first man's eyes, which were dull and lifeless. Ida's heart went out to the man as she questioned him.

"Did you have the disease called smallpox?" she asked.

"Yes," he replied.

"And did you go blind then?"

Once again the answer was yes.

Ida shook her head. "There is nothing I can do for you," she said. "Blindness from smallpox is permanent."

The second man, who had also had smallpox received the same disappointing news, but the third man had not had the disease. Ida stared hopefully into his eyes, which were badly scarred. Soon the man's story came tumbling out.

"I lost my sight when I had a fever," the man said. "The temple priest told my wife to grind up some glass and mix it with cayenne pepper and oil and rub the mixture into my eyes. It hurt a great deal, but I endured it because the priest said that the gods would grant me my eyesight back. But it has not worked. Can you restore it to me?"

Ida sighed and turned to Dr. Carol. It was a rude introduction to the despair and ignorance that lay all around them.

"I am sorry. There is nothing I can do for any of you," she said. "Some forms of blindness are curable, but not the types you have."

"Are you sure you can do nothing, Ammal?" the first man asked. "We do not have much money, but we are willing to give you all we have. Only restore our sight to us."

"I am sorry," Ida repeated quietly. "There is nothing I can do."

The drive home was somber. Ida thought about the immense needs in the villages beyond Vellore. Yes, she could use Dr. Carol and a thousand more like her before the need would be met!

Two months after Carol's arrival, the governor of Madras officially opened the Cole Dispensary and Medical Ward. The impressive, two-story building had a wide entranceway flanked by ornate wrought iron. Just walking through the waiting room left Ida feeling serene—until patients began crowding into it.

Even with the opening of the new ward, it seemed that the need for more beds grew quicker. This was because when the hospital was first opened, many of the women were so frightened that they had to be coaxed to come. Now that the hospital had so many successful operations behind it and a reputation for being welcoming and caring, women flocked to it. This meant that there was always plenty for everyone to do.

Few of Ida's staff ever considered leaving. They were as dedicated to helping the women of India as Ida was. By now Annie had been faithfully working with Ida for twenty-three years, and Gertrude for eight years. Mrs. Scudder had been Ida's faithful support since Ida's father died, and even Mrs. Gnanammal, the first pharmacist, was still there, working alongside Salomi, who had started out as the Scudders' housemaid and was now a trained pharmacist herself.

Ida relied on each person's fulfilling his or her role, and everyone did it willingly and cheerfully. The patients, few of whom had ever had anything to do with Christianity before, noticed the dedication of the staff. One day a Muslim woman was admitted to the hospital during a malaria seizure. When she recovered, she was embarrassed that she had been seen writhing on the floor and flailing at the nurses. She apologized to Ida for her behavior. Then a thought struck her. "Tell me!" she demanded, grabbing Ida's hand. "Tell me, why didn't you lose your temper with me when I went out of my mind?"

Before Ida could answer, a Hindu woman from the next bed sat up and smiled. "Don't you know?" she chided the Muslim woman. "That's what their God is like, long-suffering and slow to anger."

Ida nodded. She could not have said it better herself.

Many encouraging incidents like this occurred along the way. Ida would need more of them, though, because in February, Annie became ill. Her skin was yellow, and she had a high fever. As much as Ida hated to face it, there was only one diagnosis—cholera.

As Ida sat by Annie's side, she thought of all the good times she and Annie had shared. She recalled their antics at Northfield Seminary, the personal letters they had exchanged, the way Annie had teased Ida about being a missionary, and how Gertrude had provided the money for Annie to join her in India at the beginning. Annie had been there when Ida wept for her father and when she struggled with the overwhelming needs of the hospital. Now Ida fought desperately to save her friend's life. She gave Annie saline injections, and she and two other doctors spent fifty-six hours sitting by Annie's bed. But it was no use. Annie was slipping away from life. Her last words were, "Finish the building." In true Vellore style, right up to the end, Annie's thoughts were about expanding the facility.

The funeral service was a huge affair, a testament to the hundreds of women who had come to know Annie as their friend in the twenty-four years she had served at Vellore. When she first started visiting the women in their *zenanas*, very few of them were open to her. Before she died, not a house in the whole of Vellore did not welcome Annie to visit.

The following days were lonely for Ida. Annie's death made her feel old too, and at fifty-three Ida wondered how many years of service she had left.

In April Ida knew she needed a rest, and once again she headed for the hills of Kodaikanal. She had always found solace there, and now she had another reason to go. She had purchased eight acres of property there. To Ida it was a scenic delight, and it had cost her only one hundred dollars. She called the new property Hill Top and planned to build her own bungalow on it one day.

Once she arrived at Kodaikanal, Ida found that she could not remain idle for long. She drew up plans for a house at Hill Top, and with a generous gift from Gertrude, she began the project. It was a painfully slow process, though. Everything had to be hauled to the site, four miles above the town, by bullock cart.

Many of the other missionaries thought the task was foolish, but Ida did not care. For once she was able to build just what she wanted without worrying about committees and rules. Her imagination ran wild as she planned formal gardens with rockeries and trellises, and informal ones with masses of brightly colored flowers and apple trees. Whenever she could, Ida went to the building site to dream and direct the project. She took her mother up to the property several times to see it, but Mrs. Scudder suffered from rheumatism, and the bone-jarring road was difficult for her to cope with.

Sophia Scudder did not live to see the house at Hill Top completed. She died in her sleep on August 30, 1925. She had spent sixty-three of her eighty-six years in India and had touched many thousands of lives during that time. Even though Ida had watched her mother grow old, she was still devastated by her death. It seemed so strange that she was not there to greet Ida when she came in for lunch or ready to sit and talk at the end of a long, discouraging day.

Half of Vellore lined the streets as Sophia Scudder's casket was driven from the church to the cemetery. It was a moving sight for Ida to see so many people, Muslims, Hindus, and Christians, men and women, all standing silently in honor of her mother. The fact that they were willing to stand side by side was a tribute to the impact the gospel had had on the town.

The year ended on a happier note. It was Ida's silver jubilee. As hard as it was to believe, twenty-five years had passed since Ida had returned to Vellore to take her place as a doctor beside her father. The medical college designated her fifty-fifth birthday "College Day," and many of her old students came back to help Ida celebrate.

It was a time of great satisfaction for Ida. By now four classes of doctors—seventy students in all—had graduated from the college and spread themselves around India. Twenty-eight of them worked in mission hospitals, twenty-three in government hospitals, nine in rural villages, and five in child welfare centers; two were in private practice; and one was in New York doing postgraduate work. The last two, Ebbie Gnanamuthu and Kamala Vytbilingam, were on Ida's staff.

Twenty-five years had whisked by with its challenges and triumphs. Ida now had a medical school, a nursing school, and a large hospital, but still there was much more to be done. Ida found herself wondering what her next challenge would be.

Chapter 13

A Large Garden to Water

He has accepted the invitation, and he's coming!" Ida announced to her latest class of students in 1927. A general twitter of excitement filled the room. It was not often that a man came to address the students and staff, and perhaps only once in a lifetime it was a man like this. The man was Mahatma Gandhi, the most controversial man in India. He wore nothing but a coarsely woven loincloth and a string around his neck, and he preached nonviolent opposition to the British government and self-sufficiency for the people of India.

Many English people in the area turned up their noses when word spread that Ida intended to have Gandhi speak to her students and staff, but Ida did not care. She was as interested in meeting him as anyone, and she wanted him to see and understand the work of the medical school and hospital.

Gandhi arrived at Vellore in a red motorcar piled high with hand-woven towels, tablecloths, bedspreads, and saris, which like the hand-woven loincloth he wore, had all been made by poor Indian women as a means to support their families. As he stepped from the car to greet Ida, she was suddenly aware of what a strange sight they must be. Gandhi was a folk hero, and everyone who could be spared from his or her studies or duties was waiting for him in a ward that had been emptied of beds for the occasion. Four hundred people in all were crowded into the space to hear him speak.

Gandhi sat cross-legged on a table, and Ida sat on a chair next to the table. Gandhi spoke for only a few minutes, urging the students to serve others with a simple heart and to resist becoming proud when they gained recognition. When the talk was over, Ida showed her guest around the hospital complex, which by now consisted of an administration building, the Cole Dispensary, the children's hospital, a maternity and gynecological block, and a beautiful, white-domed chapel. The crowds thronged after Gandhi, bowing and kissing his feet whenever Ida stopped to point something out to him.

Ida and Gandhi had a private meeting together afterward, and Gandhi extolled the virtues of helping poor women to become self-sufficient through spinning and weaving homemade cloth such as he was wearing. Ida agreed. Her mother had started such a program nearly thirty years before in Vellore, teaching the lowest caste women to spin and weave.

Unfortunately Gandhi was not able to return to Vellore for the most exciting day in its history—March 5, 1927, the day the Vellore Medical School Hospital was officially opened. The entire town was caught up in the event. Bridges were whitewashed, roads were swept, and garlands and streamers hung around the railway station. Viscount Goschen, the governor of Madras, came to open the new facility. When he arrived, he had no way of being aware of the last-minute rush that had preceded his arrival. All he saw were wards of patients and attentive nurses in a clean, airy hospital.

Two thousand people—one thousand of them women—showed up for the grand opening. This was gratifying to Ida. Only a few years before, many of the women had not been outside of their *zenanas* except in heavily curtained bandies. Now here they were in public, gathering to celebrate the opening of the new hospital.

Throughout the dedication service, Ida thought about her grandfather, Dr. John Scudder I. Although she had never met him, she had read his journals. As a result she knew that just over one hundred years before he had stood on this same spot where they were sitting now and prayed that God would send a dozen laborers to meet the spiritual and medical needs of Vellore. Ida got goosebumps as she looked out over the crowd. This was the fulfillment of her grandfather's prayers.

With the new hospital up and running, it was time for Ida to take another furlough. This time Gertrude begged her to spend at least part of her time doing something relaxing. She even offered to pay for it if Ida would just tell her what kind of break she would enjoy. Ida chose to go somewhere she had never been before, north to Kashmir. Gertrude's plan called for the two of them to hire a houseboat and relax on one of the majestic lakes in Kashmir, but Ida had other plans altogether. She was ready for adventure!

Ida hired Ali Goosani, a famous guide, to lead her and Gertrude up into the Himalayan mountains, where they trekked across glaciers and to the tops of mountain peaks and ridges. While Ida loved the exhilarating climb up into the mountains, Gertrude was not so eager. Often she had to be carried in a *danty*, a chair slung from a pole and carried between two laborers. At times the trail was narrow and treacherous, and while Ida strode on ahead, Gertrude closed her eyes in fear for her life. She prayed that the laborers would bear her safely across snow bridges and along narrow ridge tracks with steep drops of hundreds of feet on either side.

Three months later Ida had hiked over five hundred miles through the Himalayas, and she was sad when that part of her furlough came to an end. She declared it to be the most relaxing vacation she had ever spent. Gertrude, on the other hand, confided that she was glad to have made it out alive.

The two women traveled on to Europe, where Ida spent a month in Vienna attending various medical conferences and observing the latest techniques being used for operations. From there it was on to Prague, Berlin, Dresden, and Paris before sailing to England and then across the Atlantic Ocean to the United States.

Many things had changed since Ida's last visit to the United States. The roads now seemed to be crowded with cars, the music was jaunty, the hemlines of women's dress had gone up, and people seemed carefree and prosperous.

Ida met many of her family members while she was in the United States, but when she added it up, she found that just as many of her family now lived in India as in the United States. After a whirlwind tour organized by Lucy Peabody, Ida was ready to go back home to India herself. She had new techniques to try on her patients and the diamond jubilee of her father and uncles coming to work in India as doctors to preside over in January 1930.

It was a huge affair—part family reunion and part medical conference. Ida's cousin Lew Scudder came with his son Galen. Her brother Henry and his wife, Margaret, were also there, along with her brother Walter, his wife, Nell, and their son Dr. John Scudder IV and his wife, Dorothy. Her brother John's daughters Maude and Nelle were there too. All of them were now missionaries to India. Her cousin Dixie, the idol of her youth, was also in attendance. She was an old woman by now, but she had finally been granted her wish and had spent the last several years touring the poorest villages in South India and living in a tent. It was a wonderful time for Ida, filled with laughter and memories.

In the evenings serious medical conversations were held. After all, some of the best doctors in India were together in one place. And time after time the conversation turned to the one disease that seemed to defeat them all—leprosy.

More than a million people in India suffered from the disease. Some of those with leprosy begged in the streets and in the railway stations, while others tried to hide the telltale light patches that developed on the skin and to go about their lives. But as the feet and hands of a leper slowly lost their feeling, the only thing a doctor could do to treat them was to amputate infected and ulcerated fingers and toes. No one seemed to know much about where the disease came from or how it was caught and passed on. Ida longed for the day when doctors would find the key to understanding and curing leprosy.

A year later another Dr. Scudder arrived in Vellore. This time Ida was delighted to welcome her niece and namesake, Ida Belle Scudder. Ida Belle had graduated from medical school and had written to offer her services to the hospital. She arrived in 1931 and set right to work alongside her aunt. To avoid confusion, everyone began calling Ida Auntie Ida and Ida Belle Dr. Ida. This suited Ida fine. At sixty years of age, she was happy to be honorary aunt to hundreds of people.

Ida pressed on with new projects: the building of an X-ray block at the hospital and the equipping of a new ambulance for the Roadsides. But fear was growing in the back of Ida's mind. Lucy's recent letters warned of a financial downturn in the United States. It was so bad that people were calling it the Great Depression, and it was affecting everyone. Men were without jobs, and women were making a pot of soup last three days. Lucy wrote that even though she and the other women were working as hard as they could to raise funds, the dollar donations they used to receive had now turned to pennies.

It did not take long for this falloff in donations to be felt at Vellore. Gertrude was a genius at making every rupee stretch as far as possible, but even she had met her match. The food budget was cut, salaries were reduced, and one branch hospital closed altogether.

These changes pained Ida greatly. She tried to be hopeful, but her hopes were dashed completely one day in October 1937 when she casually opened the latest edition of the *Madras Mail* newspaper. It was a small paragraph but one that would change Ida's vision forever. It stated that the new Indian Ministry of Public Health was closing all medical schools that were not affiliated with the University of Madras. The medical school in Vellore had been granting a licensed medical practitioner's diploma, whereas the University of Madras offered a longer medical degree.

Ida gasped when she read the paragraph. She could hardly believe it. Her students were some of the best medical students in the whole Madras area. But what did that matter if the government was discontinuing the issuing of diplomas?

Ida invited the surgeon general, Dr. Rajan, to meet with her at Vellore. He was very courteous and admired Ida's achievement of 229 graduates. But he could not see any hope for the school's continuation.

"The buildings are fine," Dr. Rajan told Ida, "but you lack adequate staff to qualify to affiliate with the University of Madras medical program. You would need twelve additional professors, each with higher credentials than anyone on your staff at present. And the hospitals would need more equipment, three new laboratories, and how many beds did you say you have?"

Ida dreaded answering him for fear of what he would say next. "Two hundred sixty eight," she mumbled.

"Yes, well, that's another problem," Dr. Rajan said apologetically. "You would need at least five hundred beds."

Ida tried to remain gracious for the rest of Dr. Rajan's visit, but she hardly heard a word more. She had heard enough! In the midst of a depression, the work at Vellore would have to find a way to double its income or her beloved medical school for women would be lost.

Ida hardly knew where to turn. Everyone was already sacrificing and working as hard as she possibly could to keep things going. And for the first time in her life, Ida fell into deep despair. She could see no way through the problem that confronted her, and neither could anyone else she spoke to.

While Ida was still in the depths of despair, one of the first-year medical students, Annamma, knocked timidly on her door. Ida invited her in.

"I am sorry to disturb you," Annamma said, "but I had a very strange dream last night, and I wanted to tell you about it."

Ida poured a cup of tea for her student. "I am not Daniel the interpreter," she said, "but go ahead and tell me what you dreamed."

"I dreamed," Annamma began, "that I was in a beautiful garden filled with all the flowers you could imagine, and in the middle of the garden was a well. Around the well were many water jugs of all sizes. In the dream I needed water, so I picked up a large jar. I decided it was too heavy, and so I put it down again and chose a smaller one to collect my water in. When I had filled the smaller jar, I noticed that many of the flowers in the garden were dying, so I started watering them. Finally I came to one particularly beautiful flower, but when I started to pour water on it, not a drop was left. I sat down and wept, wishing I had chosen the larger jar after all."

Annamma looked into Ida's eyes. "It was a strange dream, wasn't it? I have no idea why I felt I needed to tell you about it."

"Well, thank you," Ida replied. "I don't know what it means, either."

As the day unfolded, Ida thought about the dream many times—the large, heavy jar being able to water the most flowers, and the poor flower that missed out because Annamma had picked the jar she thought she could carry more easily.

By that evening Ida wanted to be alone in her room. She picked up her journal and wrote:

First ponder then dare. Know your facts. Count the cost. Money is not the important thing. What you are building is not a medical school. It is the Kingdom of God. Don't err on the side of being too small. If this is the will of God that we should find some way to keep the college open. It has to be done.

Ida underlined the last sentence. When she put down the pen she had a new determination. She would not choose the small jar just because it was easy to carry. God had given her a large garden to water, and she would shoulder the load and do whatever it took to bring the college up to the necessary standard. Somehow, she told herself, there had to be a way, and she would find it.

Chapter 14

A Coeducational College

A month later Ida welcomed a visitor to Vellore—
Dr. Fredrick Hume, an English church leader
who represented a union of denominations from
that country. He was on a three-month tour of India
looking for a place to start a medical school for men.
Of course he had read about the government's new
set of rules for colleges, and he was just as worried
as Ida was about how to meet this new challenge.

After Ida showed the doctor around, she proudly
described all that had been achieved at the hospital.
They were delivering over one thousand babies a
year, performing over four thousand operations, and
seeing thirty-six thousand patients at the Roadsides
and branch clinics. And when she told him that her
medical school students had the highest pass rate of

any medical school in the Madras region, Dr. Hume's eyes lit up.

"This is the place for our college! We have been thinking the wrong way. We don't need a men's college, we need a coeducational college," he exclaimed. "What do you say, Dr. Scudder? Think of all that we could accomplish if we joined forces."

Ida did not know what to say. Inviting men into the women's medical college? It seemed a strange idea. But over the next few weeks, the idea grew on her. Perhaps this was God's answer to the problem. Perhaps the "bigger jar" she was meant to pick up was responsibility for both men and women. After all, India was changing fast. A generation had passed since Ida had returned to India with the dream of providing medical care for women, and in that generation many of the cultural taboos against women had been dropped. Many women now saw themselves as equal with men, and that had always been Ida's dream—equality for women, not segregation from men for its own sake.

Ida continued to ponder the idea, glad that Lucy would be arriving before Christmas. Ida thought that Lucy would be a good person to discuss the idea with, since she had played such a vital role in the birth and ongoing work of the medical school.

When Lucy arrived, Ida was delighted to show her through all of the facilities that she had helped raise the money for. But for some reason Ida found it awkward to bring up the idea of inviting men into the medical college, and when she did, she soon understood why.

"You can't be serious!" Lucy gasped. "It was you who came to the United States and told us of the special needs of Indian women, how they would rather die than go to a male doctor. We have worked so hard to make this an all-women's affair—with women doctors, nurses, and students. How could you think of throwing it all away?"

"I..." Ida sputtered.

Lucy sailed on without giving Ida time to finish her sentence.

"And who is this Dr. Hume, anyway? I'll tell you what he is—an opportunist. He tours all of India and finds that you are the one with the million-dollar buildings, and next thing he wants to take them over."

Lucy then softened her voice, and she put her arm around Ida. "Look, dear. I know you are very worried about the future of the medical school, but we will find a way to raise the money. Don't give in and let men take this place over and make it their own."

This time Ida did not attempt to say anything. Lucy had certainly let her know how she felt. The problem was, Ida did not agree with her. If opening up the medical college to men meant that they could continue educating hundreds of women, she felt it was worth the trade-off.

Ida did not raise the subject again with Lucy, preferring to talk about the many wonderful things that were happening in and around Vellore. However, before Lucy went home, the matter had to be broached one last time. Again Lucy was unmoving, declaring that she would not stand by and watch men *steal* the school from the women of India.

For her part, Ida decided to let things settle down before considering the emotional topic again. She was thankful to have a big celebration to plan to take her mind off the matter. Gertrude was turning eighty. Ida arranged for a huge birthday cake to be made, and eighty candles were placed on it. One by one the party attendees came forward and blew out one of the candles as they thanked Gertrude for all she had done for them personally and for the work at Vellore.

Looking back over the twenty-three years that Gertrude had lived in Vellore, Ida was amazed at all of the things that she had financed. Gertrude was largely responsible for the tuberculosis sanatorium, a children's home, a branch hospital, and the salaries of a number of lecturers at the medical school. In addition she had paid for the complete education of eight of the school's students. At the birthday party, Ida said a prayer of thanks for her friend who had left a comfortable life in New York City to make a new home for herself in India.

The challenges and trials of the work continued for Ida. Lucy was back in the United States agitating for the all-female medical school to continue, but the money needed to upgrade the school did not come. This was partly because World War II had burst onto the scene, focusing people's attention elsewhere.

In May 1941 Ida decided to make a trip back to the United States, despite the fact that German U-boats were prowling the Atlantic Ocean and sinking ships indiscriminately. At age seventy Ida hardly felt up to the task, nor did eighty-one-year-old Gertrude Dodd. But the two elderly women decided they must make a final attempt to save the medical school.

Despite the presence of German U-boats, they arrived safely in the United States. There Ida fell into her old pattern of campaigning. She spoke three or four times a day to anyone who would listen to her pleas. Even though the United States was at war, many people were interested in Ida's story, and it surprised her to find how famous she had become. *Reader's Digest* wrote a story about her and the forty-two members of her family who over four generations had given more than a thousand years of missionary service in India.

As Ida spoke about Vellore, the idea of men entering the medical school was never far from her mind. Nor did Lucy allow Ida to forget the situation. She finally wrote to Ida and pressed her for an answer. Ida cringed as she read the letter.

> You must tell us where you stand before we go out for more appeals. Some people say you favor this cooperation with the men. If you and the majority of the board wish this coeducational work and desire to turn our plant and endowment over to the men who

have not done one single thing to help us, of course the charter can be legally changed and the board can give up and move out and let the men take charge!

It was an impassioned letter, just as impassioned as the one Ida soon received from her niece Ida Bella. "Aunt Ida," it began, "we must not put off any longer. Vellore must say yes to this development, because if we try to go on as a women's college only, we'll never do it."

As much as Ida hated to do it, she had to make a decision and announce it. She knew she was old now, but she had to be forward looking, to think of the new India that was emerging. She asked herself what would be a better fit—an all-female Christian medical college or a coeducational college in which men and women respected each other and worked side by side for the good of the Indian people. When she asked herself this question in that way, the answer was obvious to her. She sat down and wrote a letter to Lucy, knowing that she was tearing apart their many years of friendship and the trust they had built up.

In December 1942 the decision was made to open the Vellore medical school to men. Lucy wrote one last scathing letter to Ida, but Ida kept the good of the college in her thoughts and prayed that Lucy would one day come to accept the decision gracefully.

Without the backing of Lucy and her powerful friends, Ida and Gertrude continued to crisscross the country, speaking anywhere and everywhere they could. Slowly the circle of interested people began to widen. Now that the medical school was open to both men and women, twenty denominations committed to help meet the costs of the college. Ida also received news that other groups in England, Denmark, and Australia were raising money to funnel to the project. These groups called themselves "Friends of Vellore," and they committed to pray for, promote, and give to the mission. Ida encouraged them to pray for all of India and not just Vellore.

Although the news was often sketchy, the information that did come from India was frightening. In April 1942 the Japanese had attacked India, bombing Colombo, on the island of Ceylon. The attack could not have come at a worse time, as famine was spreading over the country. Next, Japanese bombs had fallen on Madras, only one hundred miles from Vellore. Ida Belle wrote that the hospital had been told to reduce its number of patients and wait for the onslaught of casualties from the war. Thankfully, war did not come to Vellore.

Then, in August, Winston Churchill, the British prime minister, had decided to take a hard line with India, fearing that it might use the war as a pretext to grab freedom from the British Empire. Mahatma Gandhi had started a campaign to protest this action, and he and a number of India's top politicians had been thrown in jail. Rioting followed, and many government buildings were destroyed, telegraph lines torn down, and railway tracks vandalized.

Ida also received word from other Vellore missionaries who were affected by the war. One of the doctors from the hospital in Vellore, Elizabeth Miller, had been traveling to England with her husband to present to English doctors what they had learned about leprosy. In the most remote part of the Atlantic Ocean, 450 miles from St. Helena Island, a U-boat had torpedoed their ship, and they had to scramble into lifeboats. Thankfully, Elizabeth had her Girl Scout compass in her handbag, and they used it to set a course for the island. Twelve days later they were all nearly dead from thirst when a ship that was itself off course rescued them. Elizabeth wrote how everyone on the lifeboat—Muslims, Hindus, and agnostics—had all asked her husband to pray that God would intervene and save them, and He had.

The war raging around the world and its effects on Vellore and the hospital staff weighed heavily on Ida and Gertrude as they spent Christmas 1943 together in St. Petersburg, Florida. The women had another concern as well. Eighty-four-year-old Gertrude had become acutely ill, and in spite of an operation, Ida was sure she was dying. It was a long, hard vigil for Ida as she watched her friend drift in and out of consciousness. Gertrude died on January 9, 1944, and Ida had her body shipped back to New York City so that she could be buried at Collegiate Church, where they had met forty-four years before.

At the funeral Dr. Norman Vincent Peale spoke, but Ida hardly heard a word he said. She was wondering how she would get along without her helper and friend who had worked alongside her in India for twenty-eight years.

By January 26 Ida was back in Florida, continuing to publicize and raise money for the work in Vellore. She decided that this would be the best way to honor her friend, no matter how painful it felt not having Gertrude at her side.

Ida still had a long way to go to reach her goal, but she plodded on. By July 1945, just as the war was coming to a close, she had raised and sent to Vellore a sizable amount of money. It was time for her to go "home" to India. She set sail from New York on August 28, five days before Japan surrendered and World War II officially came to an end. A new day was dawning for the world and, most especially, Ida hoped, for the medical school in Vellore.

The voyage across the Atlantic Ocean and through the Mediterranean Sea took longer than anticipated. Ida was so impatient to get back to Vellore that she booked herself a seat on an airplane to go the rest of the way, from Cairo to India. When she got off the airplane, she declared, "Now that is the way to travel. I have finally found a mode of transport that's fast enough for me."

All the way from Madras to Vellore, Ida strained her eyes for glimpses of people she recognized. She was a little disappointed that she would arrive home in the middle of the night, when everyone was asleep. But her disappointment soon turned to wonder as she was driven through the gates of the medical college. As far as she could see was a line of people, all holding blazing torches. Her niece, Ida Belle, who was driving, slowed the car to a crawl, and nurses and former patients ran out to cover Ida with garlands of flowers. As Ida smelled the flowers—the frangipani, the roses, and the nasturtiums—tears sprang to her eyes.

As soon as it was light, Ida was up, eagerly touring the hospital grounds. There was a new pathology and research block, and new wings had been added to the nurses' home, the children's ward, and the administration building. Despite the war, progress had been made.

Many new staff members were at the hospital, from Australia, Ireland, England, Canada, and the United States. Ida was particularly pleased to meet Dr. Florence Nichols, the first woman psychiatrist in India. Dr. Nichols told Ida how on her arrival in India she had been at the train station in Madras. She began to despair of getting all her luggage loaded onto the train before it left for Vellore. In a panic she ran to the station master to ask what could be done. He shrugged his shoulders as if to say it was not his problem that a white woman had brought so many things with her to India. Then he casually asked, "Where are you going, anyway?"

Florence replied, "The Vellore Christian Medical College."

At the mention of these words, the station master snapped to attention. "In that case the train will not leave until all your baggage is on board," he said emphatically.

"But...I might hold up the train for ten minutes. Some of my bags are still in the car that brought me to the station."

"No matter," the station master said, coming out from behind his booth and taking Dr. Nichols by the arm. "I said the train will not leave without you."

The station master escorted Dr. Nichols to her compartment and kept watch until her last bag was safely stowed on the train. Then he waved a flag at the engineer. As the train began to chug away, he waved at Florence through the open window of the carriage and yelled, "Dr. Scudder saved my life. I fell off a horse, and she operated on me. Greet her for me and tell her there is nothing I would not do for her and her hospital."

Ida's eyes misted over as she heard the story. It was good to be home again with the people whom she loved and served. However, there were so many changes that Ida had to keep reminding herself she had been away for four long years. Dr. Robert Cochrane, a Scotsman with more qualifications than Ida, was now principal of the new coeducational medical school. Ida had known that she would not get the job; she did not have enough degrees to satisfy the Indian government. Besides, she was now seventy-four years old. Her role had changed, and she was happy to accept it. Ida resolved to do whatever she could to help get the medical college ready for the inspections that would determine its fitness to be a part of the Indian university system.

Now that Ida did not have the daily weight of running the college resting on her shoulders, she felt a new spring in her step. There was so much else to do.

Chapter 15

Time to Retire

When Ida Scudder turned seventy-five in December 1945, she was still working full days. When Dr. Cochrane went on a business trip to England that same month, Ida was asked to step in once again and become the acting principal and director of the medical college and hospital. She accepted the responsibility with delight. Despite her age, Ida threw herself into her old role. She spent the mornings making hospital rounds and the afternoons studying the budget for the new building projects. In the evenings she hosted small groups of first-year medical students, both men and women, so that she could get to know them all.

When Dr. Cochrane returned in late January, Ida handed control back to him. She knew it was now time to do some serious thinking. She was already ten years beyond retirement age for Reformed Church missionaries, and she knew she could not keep up the strenuous pace of working in the hospital for too long. Besides, when she was at the hospital, many of the patients and staff instinctively looked to her instead of Dr. Cochrane for guidance and instruction. The fact was inescapable: it was time for her to retire.

Ida's four years spent in the United States had firmly convinced her that her heart lay in India. Not only had she been born there, but also she had lived there for over fifty years. To her it was home. Ida announced her intention to retire in August 1946. Her plan was to move permanently to Hill Top and live there.

At her retirement celebration, Ida insisted that everyone remain positive and look on the bright side of things. She was concerned that if her staff starting telling her how much they would miss her, she would break down in tears for the evening. She happily reminded everyone that, unlike the old days, when it was an arduous train and mule journey to get to Kodaikanal, now it was less than a day away by car. Ida told everyone that she was planning to enlarge her garden at Hill Top, and she invited everyone to visit her.

Ida did not have many belongings to transport up the winding road to her new permanent home. What she did transport were mainly items of furniture that had belonged to her parents and gifts she had been given over the years.

Hill Top was beautiful in August, and Ida settled down to a well-disciplined regimen. In the morning she wrote letters to old students and the many "Friends of Vellore" groups that were springing up around the world. Then, in the afternoon, she and her gardener, Chinnekin, tackled the mammoth task of enlarging the garden. Ida also decided to build a waterfall. The fact that she lived on top of a mountain and there was no water nearby did not deter her! In the evenings she read medical journals and entertained friends.

People flocked to Hill Top to stay with Ida, who welcomed them all. Sometimes the house resembled a hotel, and more than once Ida had to lock herself in the pantry to find a quiet place to write.

During summer, when the population of Kodaikanal swelled in number, it was nothing for Ida to have forty or fifty guests in one day, all wanting to talk with her and tour the beautiful gardens. Everyone marveled at the waterfall, which was a feat of ingenuity and engineering, and ate delicious, fresh meals prepared by Ida's cook, Sebastian.

The following year, on August 15, 1947, India became an independent nation, and the new government showed just how much progress Indian women had made since Ida had arrived back in the country for good at the turn of the century. A woman was appointed minister of health and another the governor of West Bengal Province.

Much to Ida's delight, that same year an Indian woman took over the leadership of the hospital and medical school. She was Dr. Hilda Lazarus, a long-time supporter of the work at Vellore. When Dr. Cochrane resigned from his position, Dr. Lazarus was appointed to replace him. It was the fulfillment of all Ida had worked for—Indian women helping themselves and each other. Ida went to the ceremony to welcome Dr. Lazarus to her new position, and she herself was welcomed back with open arms. "Don't stay away so long next time!" everyone pleaded.

After that Ida did go down to Vellore more often, and every time she went, she marveled at the medical advances being made. She was particularly impressed with Dr. Rambo, an eye specialist who was pioneering a new concept called an eye camp. As head of the Schell Eye Hospital he, like Ida before him, had become very frustrated with the number of incurable cases of blindness he saw. "Why do they wait until it is too late before they come for help?" he bemoaned. Then Dr. Rambo came up with the idea of an eye camp, a kind of specialized Roadside to deal with people with sight problems.

Ida was invited to go along on the first eye camp. She was so eager to do so that she was waiting outside Dr. Rambo's bungalow an hour before it was time to leave. A "teller of good news" had been sent out to the towns and villages around Gudiyattam several days before to tell anyone with eye disease or blindness that a medical team was coming to give free examinations. If a doctor determined that a person would benefit from an eye operation, the surgery would be done right there the same day.

No one had any idea how many people would respond to such an offer, but as the car neared the tiny branch hospital, the driver had to slow down to a crawl. Over three hundred people were crowding around the gate. Ida helped Dr. Rambo and his team as they set up tables and organized the patients into long lines. One at a time, the people knelt in front of the doctor to have their eyes examined. There was no hope for some of the patients, but many others could have their eyesight saved or restored. These patients had a tag sewn onto their shirts or saris telling their condition and the type of operation they needed.

At the end of a very long morning, the totals were tallied. Fifty-seven people, including many babies and toddlers, would benefit from cataract operations. It was far too many for the branch hospital to cope with, but a mill owner offered his warehouse as an operating theatre. Ida helped as the warehouse was transformed. Operating tables were set up, and a number was added to each patient's tag, telling the staff the order in which each patient would be operated on.

All of the patients formed a long line, and the processing began. The first nurse shaved a patient's eyebrows, the second gave anesthetic, and then Dr. Rambo operated. Following the operation a third nurse bandaged up the eye, and then a fourth nurse laid the patients on matting at the far end of the warehouse. Each patient was then watched over while he or she came out from under the anesthetic.

The whole process went like clockwork, and together the members of the team could do six operations an hour. When night fell, there were still many patients to go, so kerosene lanterns were lit and the work continued. Someone offered to take Ida back to Vellore to rest, but she would not hear of it. Things were much too exciting where she was!

When the final surgery was completed, sometime after midnight, fifty-seven bandaged people lay in two neat rows on the warehouse floor. The medical team left behind a cook to supply the patients with food and a nurse to provide care for them for a week, after which the medical team would return to take off the bandages.

When Ida finally did get to bed, she was unable to sleep. She kept thinking of all the lives that had been changed that day, all the children who could now learn to read, all the women who could now cook and sew for their families, and all the men who could provide for their own families once again. Fifty-seven operations had been carried out that day, but better yet, Dr. Rambo planned to hold eye camps twice a week.

A few months after the first eye camp, Ida once again descended from Hill Top, this time to meet a brilliant young surgeon named Paul Brand. Like Ida, Dr. Brand had been born to missionary parents in India and had come back to help change the lot of the poorest people. He had chosen a challenge close to Ida's heart—leprosy. The Vellore Christian Medical College had just entered a partnership with the new government to research the sulphone drugs that were showing such promise in the treatment of the disease.

Ida had come to witness the results of Dr. Brand's first operation to restore movement to the hand of a twenty-four-year-old Hindu man. The man's hand had been paralyzed by leprosy. Ida listened as Dr. Brand modestly explained that he had discovered one set of arm muscles that were unaffected when a patient became paralyzed. The new operation, which Dr. Brand was pioneering, attempted to transplant parts of those good muscles and tendons into the "clawed" hand so that it would work again.

The only sound that could be heard in the room was the rhythmic sawing of plaster as the cast was removed from the man's hand and arm. The bandages underneath were meticulously unwound, and then Dr. Brand massaged the patient's hand. Finally he stepped back so that Ida could see.

"Go ahead and use it," Dr. Brand said to the Hindu man.

The young man held his hand to his face and then slowly began to wiggle his fingers. He stared at his hand as if it belonged to someone else, and then he reached down and gingerly picked up a piece of the plaster cast.

A cheer went up from the nurses and doctors in the room. Like Ida, they all knew they had witnessed a medical milestone.

The young man shook with sobs as he turned to Dr. Brand. "This new hand you give me," he said, "is not mine. It belongs to your God, who made this miracle possible."

Ida wiped tears from her eyes at the man's response, glad that she had lived long enough to see significant developments in the field of treating leprosy.

Much to Ida's delight, Dr. Brand stayed on at Vellore and performed many more such operations, finally giving leprosy patients hope for the future.

It was not the future, however, but the past that everyone was contemplating three years later when Vellore celebrated a special day, January 1, 1950— exactly fifty years since Ida Scudder had returned to India to start her medical work.

The governor of Madras and his wife arrived to attend the ceremony. "You are one of those rare spirits," the governor told Ida from the platform, "that is sent to the earth once in a generation."

And what had Ida accomplished in that generation? She had started with one housemaid to help her as she built a medical empire. Now there were forty-three doctors on the medical college staff and forty-four on the hospital roster. Over half were Indian doctors, and many of them were graduates of the medical college. The small clinic Ida had opened after her father's death had grown into a 544-bed hospital staffed by 108 nurses and 174 nursing students. Two hundred doctors had graduated from the medical college, and two hundred seventy-five nurses from the nurses' training school. Now they were spread all over India and beyond. Ida thought of the times she had wanted to give up, but the recollection of those three dead women and their babies had spurred her on.

Yes, God is good, Ida thought. *He has done more than I could ever have hoped or dreamed.*

For Ida there was one crowning moment to the celebration. The medical college had been on probation since it had become a coeducational institution and money was raised to upgrade both the buildings and the faculty. On the day that the governor of Madras arrived, so did a special message from the Madras State Office. It was official: the government recognized the permanent affiliation of the Vellore Christian Medical College to the University of Madras.

This was the best gift Ida could have hoped for. It meant that the medical college was at last on a secure footing. Ida had been right to endorse the move to open the school's doors to men. It had saved the college and recognized the changing nature of Indian society. As Ida listened to Dr. Lazarus speak, she smiled as she thought about how this petite woman was the leader of not only the female students but also the male students. The men hadn't stolen the school away, as Lucy had predicted.

Ida should have expected that there would be other tributes to her fifty years of service, but she was still horrified when the citizens of Vellore announced that they had raised enough money to erect a bronze statue of her in the town.

"Oh, don't do that!" Ida exclaimed at the news. "Do something of value. Something for the hospital."

In the end, when Ida continued to protest the planned statue, the money was put toward building a new road opposite the hospital. Nothing, however, could stop the people of Vellore from calling it the "Dr. Ida Scudder Road."

The first time Ida drove over the road she laughed. How wonderful it would have been to have had roads like this when she went out on the first Roadsides. She thought of the springless bandies she covered hundreds of miles in and the one-cylinder Peugeot that sputtered its way along the rutted roads.

At times throughout the jubilee year, Ida allowed herself to reminisce. But as always, she was much more comfortable thinking ahead to the next challenge.

Chapter 16

Her Legacy Remained Alive

Ida continued to visit Vellore and watch the new developments taking place there. On one visit in February, she was driven sixteen miles to Kavanur, where the hospital was opening a new rural health center. Ida had followed this project carefully, and she was pleased with what they were doing. The health center was staffed by third-year nursing students, who took turns living there for a month at a time. During their stay the students treated patients and helped the local people understand basic health concepts so that they could prevent illness. They gave health talks to mothers and gathered men to build better toilet systems and make new stoves that did not smoke up their homes. They also worked with the local midwives, encouraging them to use clean instruments and cloths.

Ida's next trip down from Hill Top was to tour the new Leprosy Rehabilitation Center, with its neat row of whitewashed huts. This was Dr. Brand's special project. In the time since Ida had watched him perform his first hand surgery, he had perfected the art of restoring the use of feet as well as hands. But because of the stigma of leprosy, even with hands and feet that once again functioned, many of the patients were unable to find work. Because they were lepers, no one wanted to employ those on whom Paul Brand had operated. The rehabilitation center was designed to address this situation, training twenty-four men at a time to do carpentry, masonry, toy making, and painting. This also was something that delighted Ida. What could be better than helping a man back onto his feet and then helping him find a way to once again look after himself and his family?

As 1950 drew to a close, another great celebration was held. This time it was not to commemorate Ida's fifty years in India but to celebrate her eightieth birthday. Ida traveled down from Hill Top on December 6 to give herself some time to "rest" before the event. Of course she did not rest. Ida busied herself visiting the wards and catching up on news from her past staff and students.

When the sun rose on December 9, Ida was wide awake. *I am eighty years old today,* she thought as she lay in bed. *If only I had another eighty years to spend serving India!*

From the moment Ida got out of bed, she was treated like royalty. The students had made her a beautiful "birthday chair," a high-backed wooden chair covered with woven flowers that Ida sat on as she listened to speech after speech from colleagues, servants, students, residents of Vellore, and former patients.

The organizing committee had saved the best until last. At six in the evening, hundreds of people gathered on the nurses' badminton court. Ida was escorted onto a makeshift platform by Vellore's police training college band. She gasped as she caught sight of a huge, six-layer birthday cake that glowed with eighty colored lights.

Ida sat down on yet another floral birthday chair, and then twenty-two of the staff children paraded in front of her. Each child was dressed in the national costume of one of the countries or Indian provinces that had sent cash gifts for Ida's personal use. One by one the children kissed their Auntie Ida and placed in her lap a gold purse containing the amount given by the country or province that each child represented.

When the gifts were tallied, they amounted to twenty thousand dollars. Invested properly, the money would be enough to make sure that Ida lived in comfort the rest of her life. However, Ida had other ideas about what a proper investment was.

The morning following Ida's birthday, Dr. Edward Gault, the men's dean at the medical college, showed Ida the newly completed men's dorm—a primitive building with a thatched roof.

"That's no way to treat the men!" Ida chided him.

"The need was desperate," Edward apologized, "and it was all we could afford. We have more elaborate plans drawn up, and as soon as all the money comes in, we will make a start."

"Ha!" Ida exclaimed. "If I'd waited for the money to come in before I started, there wouldn't be anything here! If we want a permanent men's dorm, we need to get going. How much will it cost?"

"Around $160,000 to do it properly," Edward replied.

"I have the first $20,000 to put in," Ida said. "What better place to invest the money than in the young men of India?"

Ida thought for a moment. She had another $10,000 in a special account to go to the Vellore Hospital after she died. "Make that $30,000," she said. "Come on. Let's make the announcement and turn over the sod to begin the project this afternoon. Waiting for the money to come in, indeed!"

"I suppose we could begin with that amount of money and then stop when the money runs out and wait until we can raise more," Dr. Gault said.

"God will provide," Ida assured him. "Once you start, I am sure everything will fall into place. It always has."

That afternoon Ida dug a spade into the ground, turned the sod, and announced that the men's hostel building project was under way. Her enthusiasm was contagious. The following week one of the students made a model of the proposed men's hostel and took a photograph of it. The photograph was printed onto cards, and each card was sold for the price of a single brick. Thousands of the cards were sold. In addition, the Madras Chamber of Commerce took up the challenge and raised ten thousand dollars toward the project. Other donations came in from as far away as Australia.

On subsequent visits to Vellore, Ida watched as the three-story building rose on its foundation. The building went ahead steadily and was never once held up for lack of funds. Ida, of course, was on hand to open the new building when it was finished.

As the years passed, Ida continued to get up at 5:30 every morning and work an hour or more in her garden after breakfast. Her health continued to be excellent, so good, in fact, that she played tennis with people a quarter of her age and often beat them!

When she was eighty-two, Ida did have a minor hernia operation. It was the first time she had been a patient on the operating table instead of standing over it, and she enjoyed the novelty of the whole event. She was given a local anesthetic and, with the use of a mirror, was able to follow the progress of the entire operation. She recovered in grand style, surrounded by fresh flowers every day and adorned with immaculately styled hair. Each morning before the visitors arrived, one of the nurses volunteered to style Ida's hair.

Ida had other novel experiences too. At eighty-five she accepted Ida Belle's invitation to go on an elephant trek into the jungle of Mysore. Merely getting up onto and down from an elephant would have put most eighty-five-year-old women off, but Ida could not wait to begin this latest adventure. It began at three in the morning, when Ida was roused from her bed at the guest house. Half an hour later both Ida Scudders were standing in front of an enormous elephant. With much pushing and shoving, Ida was positioned just behind the animal's head, with Ida Belle behind her. Soon the two women were bumping through the jungle at tree height. After ten minutes of the elephant's constant pitching, Ida announced, "This is dreadful!"

"Do you want to go back, Aunt Ida?" her niece asked sympathetically.

"Mercy, no!" Ida replied. Dreadful or not, she was having the time of her life.

The sun rose to reveal lush tropical jungle. Occasionally Ida saw deer darting away from them. It was a day she talked about with guests for months to come.

In June 1955 Ida attended the opening of the Leprosy Research Sanatorium at Karigeri. She was particularly pleased because this was a joint project with the Vellore hospital and the British Mission to Lepers, a group that encouraged Dr. Brand's experimentation with new medicines and techniques for treating leprosy.

Even though she lived at Hill Top, Ida kept up-to-date with national events. She was particularly impressed with the job Prime Minister Jawaharlal Nehru was doing in community development, and so she was delighted to be invited to a function he would be attending. It was the centenary celebration of the University of Madras, and Ida had a front-row seat. Nehru was to be the guest speaker at the event.

As the procession of dignitaries walked up the aisle, the audience remained seated, as it had been instructed to do. Everyone stayed seated, that is, except Ida Scudder.

"Do sit down, Aunt Ida," Ida Belle said, pulling on her aunt's sleeve.

"But I came here to see the prime minister, and I can't see him when I am sitting down," she explained matter-of-factly. She remained standing until the vice chancellor spotted her. He waved and stopped the procession so that he could introduce Ida to the prime minister.

Jawaharlal Nehru looked into Ida's eyes and said, "I am honored, Doctor."

Two years later, in 1957, the National Broadcasting Company in New York brought a seven-man team to Vellore. The team was filming a show called the "March of Medicine," featuring medical stories from around the world. Vellore was its only stop in India. The men found so many things to report on that they stayed for seventeen days. They filmed the leprosy rehabilitation program, the eye clinics, which by now had given ten thousand people their sight back, and the many Roadsides that still radiated out from the hospital. They finished their visit by interviewing Ida in her Hill Top garden.

By now Ida was eighty-six years old. Her shoulders were beginning to stoop, and her walk had slowed a little, but her mind was as sharp as ever. During the interview she meticulously quoted statistics on the growth of medical science in India during the fifty-seven years she had been there. Back in the United States, twenty million people watched the broadcast of the interview, many of the older ones no doubt recalling Ida's famous fundraising techniques of years gone by.

The following year Ida broke her hip, but her determination won through. Unwilling to spend the rest of her life in bed, she exercised every day and was soon up and about her beautiful garden again.

Early in 1959, sixty years after she graduated from Cornell University, Ida received an honor she was particularly proud of. The Cornell Alumni Association awarded Ida a medal of distinction. Ida's eyes misted over as she read the inscription that accompanied the medal. "In recognition of her notable contribution to medical education, public health, and international understanding. Her life of devoted service to mankind is an inspiration to all and has brought honor and acclaim to the [Cornell] medical college."

It was as if the celebrations of her life and work never ended! Following the awarding of the medal of distinction, Ida marked sixty years of service in India in January 1960. And in December that same year she would celebrate her ninetieth birthday. To mark both of these events, a large combined celebration was planned for August, after the student vacations were over.

Ida heard snippets of the events planned for the occasion. The president of India and the governor of Madras, along with the American ambassador to India, had already accepted invitations to attend. And Ida Belle was coming back early from furlough to preside over the event.

One day, three months before the celebration was due to take place, Ida went about her usual routine. She gardened in the morning, had guests for lunch, and accompanied them on a ten-mile car ride through the hills. Then after dinner she joined in a group sing-along that included her favorite hymns.

The following morning Ida awoke early feeling dizzy. It wasn't the first time she had experienced such spells, but something about this one was different.

A nurse who was staying with Ida offered to make her a cup of coffee. "It will help clear your head," she said.

"Not this time," Ida replied emphatically.

Five minutes later Ida Sophia Scudder was dead.

Later that same day, May 24, 1960, a funeral service was held in Kodaikanal, and then Ida's body was transported overnight to Vellore. The cavalcade arrived in Vellore at 7:00 A.M. to find the normally bustling town silent. No children ran to school, the market was empty, the blinds in houses were pulled down, and thousands of people lined the route, their heads bowed and their minds filled with personal memories of their Dr. Ida.

Ida's official funeral was held at 7:45 in front of the administration block, as there was no building large enough to contain the crowd. While she had died three months before the celebration of her life in India, her life was well celebrated at the funeral. An Indian man, the general superintendent of the hospital, gave the eulogy.

"Only those who can see the invisible can achieve the impossible," he said, with tears streaming down his face. "Dr. Ida Scudder has achieved the impossible through her close touch with the invisible God through her faith."

When he was finished, Dr. Carol Jameson, whom Ida had recruited to work in Vellore thirty-seven years before, read the thirteenth chapter of 1 Corinthians, the same chapter Ida had read aloud many times to her students over the years.

As Ida Scudder's coffin was placed in the hearse, the gathered crowd sang "O Love That Wilt Not Let Me Go." It was Ida's favorite hymn.

The hearse pulled slowly away from the hospital, headed for the Tamil Church, where Ida was to be buried. Doctors, students, cooks, lepers, orphans, and town dignitaries fell silently in line behind it, forming a mile-long procession.

Ida's body was buried beside her mother's grave, yet her legacy remained alive. It was reflected in the hearts of the hundreds of people who stood respectfully watching her coffin being lowered into the Indian soil, and in the thousands of people across India and around the world who had been healed and inspired by the touch of this amazing doctor.

——————————————————————

It has been over one hundred years since Ida
Scudder returned to Vellore to set up a medical
clinic for women. Today the Vellore Christian
Medical College and Hospital operates much like a
small town. It has a staff of over 5,000 people, including 596 doctors, 1,545 nurses, and 183 teaching staff.
The medical college, which Ida fought so hard to
preserve, takes in sixty students a year, with a mini-
mum of twenty-five of those being women. Fifteen
places are set aside for low-income students, and
many Christian churches in India supply scholar-
ships to these promising students.

The various hospitals and clinics serve over eighty
thousand inpatients a year and over 1.2 million outpatients. Each day ten Bible classes are held in nine
languages and broadcast throughout the complex so
that any patient can tune in and listen. Hospital chap-
lains visit and pray with 380 patients a day.

Both the hospital and the college continue the
standard of excellence that their founder set. In 2002
India Today magazine ranked the Vellore medical
college the top college in India. The hospital is known
around the world for its thorough research in the
area of tropical disease and its innovations in rural

health care, disease prevention, and community empowerment.

Friends of Vellore still meet around the world, raising money, recruiting staff, and praying for the continuing work.

In 1900 Dr. Ida Scudder came to India with the modest goal of helping the women of Vellore. Through her dedication and faith, she has left a legacy, the impact of which is still felt every year by millions of people whose bodies are healed and hearts are touched through the ministry of the hospital and medical school at Vellore.

Bibliography

Jeffery, Pauline. *Ida S. Scudder of Vellore: The Life Story of Ida Sophia Scudder*. Fleming H. Revell, 1951.

Scott, Carolyn. *The Doctor Who Never Gave Up: The Story of Ida Scudder in India*. Lutterworth Press, 1970.

Scudder, Dorothy Jealous. *A Thousand Years in Thy Light: The Story of the Scudder Missionaries of India*. Vantage Press, 1984.

Wilson, Dorothy Clarke. *Dr. Ida: The Story of Dr. Ida Scudder of Vellore*. McGraw-Hill, 1959.

Janet and Geoff Benge are a husband and wife writing team with more than thirty years of writing experience. Janet is a former elementary school teacher. Geoff holds a degree in history. Originally from New Zealand, the Benges spent ten years serving with Youth With A Mission. They have two daughters, Laura and Shannon, and an adopted son, Lito. They make their home in the Orlando, Florida, area.

CHRISTIAN HEROES: THEN & NOW are available in paperback, e-book, and audiobook formats, with more coming soon!

www.HeroesThenAndNow.com